Heroes
of the
Western Woods

Also by Ralph W. Andrews

THIS WAS LOGGING

GLORY DAYS OF LOGGING

THIS WAS SAWMILLING

REDWOOD CLASSIC

FISH AND SHIPS (co-author)

THIS WAS SEAFARING (co-author)

Heroes
of the
Western Woods

RALPH W. ANDREWS

ILLUSTRATED WITH PHOTOGRAPHS

E. P. DUTTON & COMPANY, INC.
NEW YORK, 1960

TO BARRIE

Library of Congress Catalog Card No.: 60-11868

THE RIGGER

By Charles Oluf Olsen

With steel-caulked shoes
That bite and grip,
With their laces hid
So they cannot trip;
With slicker short, for the sake of ease,
And tin pants stagged, close to the knees,
He takes the trail among the trees.

The rain comes down
With a sidelong sweep;
The branches softly sway and weep,
And make a pool where the trail is deep.
He casts a vigilant glance on high—
Overhead—where the fir-tops sigh;
The water pours from his glazed hat brim
As he looks aloft from under the rim.

He leaps a puddle and swears a bit,
At the wet and the wind
And the chill of it;
Rivulets trickle and flow and leap,
And cascade down
Where the ground is steep;
He wades through mud where the yarder stands,
And climbs to the boiler
To warm his hands;
He grabs his gloves, takes a chew of snoose,
And joins the crew

That by threes and twos
Plod out to their work through the muck and ooze.

The yarder-drums stir,
And the cables glide
Up through the high-lead and down beside;
Liquid, enveloping, yellow-brown mud,
Clings to them, covers them,
Drains in a flood
From their thread-like lengths,
As they tighten and slack
Over the road to the woods and back;
From spar-pole blocks
Comes a steady rain
Of spattering slush, as they swing and strain.

The loaders stand knee-deep
In debris and mire,
Over a sodden, smoke-blanketed fire
That sulks and sputters,
And will not burn.

The chaser sits hunched, awaiting the turn;
All his garments are slushy,
And down
From his paraffined pants
Stream small rivers of brown;
Where the sticky clay stain
From choker and chain
Dissolves in the wetness and colors the rain.

Incessant—depressing—benumbing and chill;
Drizzle and splash,
Over yard, over fill—
Above and beyond—to the end of things,
Where the vision ends
And the cloud bank clings.

CONTENTS

PAGE

FOREWORD   9

FIRST AXES IN THE REDWOODS: *California, 1846*   13

THE BIG FOUR OF MENDOCINO: *California, 1850*   20

SEA LEGS ASHORE: *Oregon, 1850*   30

TREASURE IN TREES: *Washington, 1853*   42

DAREDEVIL OF THE DOG HOLES: *California, 1870*   50

"ELLSWORTH'S FOLLY" *California, 1872*   63

BOY LOGGER OF MILL CREEK: *California, 1881*   73

BOILED BEEF AND BEANS AT DAYLIGHT:
  Washington, 1884   83

KINGS OF CONVERSE BASIN: *California, 1885*   93

BIG STEEL ON PUGET SOUND: *Washington, 1887*   102

"HUMP! YOU—BUCK!" *Washington, 1890*   108

THE GREAT SUGAR PINE CHUTE: *Oregon, 1893*   114

THE CLEAN GUY: *Oregon, 1905*   123

WHEN FORESTS WENT TO SEA: *Oregon, 1906*   133

SPRING DRIVE ON THE PIT: *California, 1906*   141

THEY HARNESSED THE WILD LOGS: *Washington, 1909*   152

RED SKY OVER HUNTING CREEK: *Washington, 1912*   162

SAMPSON OF THE TREETOPS: *Washington, 1915*   173

TRACKS TO THE CLOUDS: *Washington, 1915*   180

BOOKS FOR FURTHER READING   188

INDEX   189

ILLUSTRATIONS

FOLLOWING PAGE *32*

Grove of California redwood trees

Three days' chopping had only chipped away three feet . . .

"Twenty men with arms outstretched couldn't reach around them."

Port Gamble mill

FOLLOWING PAGE *64*

It took raw courage to enter and anchor in the dog holes on the wild Mendocino Coast.

"Ellsworth's Folly"—a successful lumber flume

Saws had to be welded end-to-end to cut the redwoods.

"It was a constant battle . . . until the bulls became tangled and the driver stopped the team."

FOLLOWING PAGE *128*

Admiralty Hall—Cyrus Walker's castle

Even Smith and Moore's bulls were bigger—to match the biggest redwoods of them all.

"They had special augers forged in Redding . . ."

". . . to slash the right-of-way through virgin timber . . ."

"At this frightful bellow, the bulls snorted, tensed, and staggered forward."

"The clean guy loved ships, like this lumber schooner sailing off the Oregon coast."

". . . a veritable whale of a log raft."

"Up out of the tangle came the log, threshing and slapping like something alive . . ."

The high climber begins his ascent to the towering crown.

"The big green crown had snapped free and was hurtling earthward . . ."

"Tracks to the clouds"

FOREWORD

THERE were probably as many heroes in West Coast logging as there were camps and sawmills. On every creek and side hill there were men as big in stature as the redwoods and firs they brought thundering to earth—men with color, spirit, inner strength, and drive. Their kinds of valor varied but they all ended up kicking their calks along the Big Skid Road in the Sky.

Every person has his own conception of what a hero should be. And those in lumbering certainly differ from those in war, skin diving, and the stock market. The ones I have chosen for this book represent my own ideas of what heroes in Western lumbering were made of and they range from the pioneer logger, with his uncanny vision, to the "Rock 'em–sock 'em" river pig. In between, the reader will find men of courage, dogged determination, and mechanical genius, most of them with a dedicated sense of self-sacrifice.

In the Big Woods, where conditions were new and ever changing, most of the loggers were green hands and the trees were the biggest anybody had ever handled. There were constant problems, decisions, and dangers. In the early days there were no easy jobs, no safety rules—but always emergencies. Fallers, buckers, donkey punchers, and bull drivers put "daylight in the swamp" by holding trouble at arm's length.

So naturally there was always someone who stood out from the rest of the working stiffs. Maybe he had an oversupply of courage with no place to use it but tight spots, and worked on the theory that his guardian angel was riding his good ear. Or he might have had an aptitude for looking at today's cut of timber and seeing tomorrow's. He might have been a man with a light in his eye that said: "I won't be here long, Buck." This was ambition other than marrying the boss's niece.

Only a few such men can appear in one book. Many who might have been included had other qualities less romantic, or possible records of them have been lost. Others are yet to be recognized as heroes, their exploits still buried in dusty cellars and behind the inarticulate tongues of men who worked with them.

The events here presented are based on actual happenings as I found them recorded or recited. There were some gaps in the accounts and these were filled in from my general knowledge of the situations. Minor characters, scenes, action, and dialogue were supplied to make the accounts complete and understandable.

For the intimate details of the chief characters portrayed I thank the men whose memories and papers I disturbed—men like camp blacksmith Charley Olsen, historian Harold Schutt, storekeeper Louis Seymour, sawmill superintendent E. J. Stewart, and lumber company historian Alder Thurman. The kind words and colorful writings of Stewart Holbrook have been a help and stimulation. I also thank the many members of historical societies and the librarians who made available to me ancient files of newspapers, lumber trade publications, and county and lumber firm histories.

Seattle 1960   RALPH W. ANDREWS

Heroes
of the
Western Woods

I

California . . . 1846

FIRST AXES IN THE REDWOODS

THE giant redwood stood apart from the others in the thick forest. The bushy top, more than two hundred feet from the ground, was bunched toward the side that faced a clearing which sloped to the river canyon. The pines and oaks beyond in the sunlight were dwarfed by the towering red-barked bulk.

On a crude scaffold, built ten feet high around the redwood, two boys stood ankle deep in chips. More chips lay in a thick circle around the swelling base of the tree. A mustached man joined the boys on the scaffold. He mopped the sweat from his forehead and sank down in one of the axed-out hollows.

"I dunno," he said with a discouraged shake of his head. "Might be she'll go over in another hour. Maybe not till tomorry. If'n we had a good saw. . . ."

The taller of the two boys smiled grimly. "It's ten days now since Dick and I started on it. We've hurried it up some since you came along to help. About all we can do now is to keep going. She'll come down sometime."

The man pulled at the trailing ends of his mustache. " 'Course the way ye boys started hackin' at her spoiled doin' a good job. Ef ye had only chopped it out on two sides instead of all around, she'd be layin' down flat afore this. Now the way ye got her, she'll come whoopin' down all of a sudding like—and in most any direction."

"We told you, Mr. Duff—we never cut a big tree down before."

The man nodded morosely. "Never needed to tell me. Ye was greenies, I could see right off. That's why I threwed in with ye when I come by and heered ye whackin' away. I ain't complainin' withal. Jest tellin'."

The three kept going, driving the heavy broadaxes into the solid red heart of the tree, chipping tiny bits out of the cavernlike walls of wood. At times they eased one set of muscles to drag a thick, unwieldy crosscut saw across the stubborn fibers and to stone-whet the twelve-inch blades of the axes.

Hunger finally stopped the work and they made supper at the campfire. The man, Wiley Duff, fed his horse as well, leading him to a creek and returning with two buckets of water. When darkness set in the three slept like exhausted animals, dreaming of ease in pleasant places. At sunup they made tea and worked for an hour before a breakfast of deer liver.

Two more hours had gone by when the great shaft shuddered ominously. The shorter, heavier boy, Jacob Harlan, was alone on the platform. He stepped quickly to the edge of it and looked up at the bushy top. There was not a breath of wind and yet the branches were swaying. His hand against the tree bark could detect a distinct tremor.

Then two sounds came at the same second—a shout from

the others on the ground and a rifle-shot crack deep within the bole of the redwood. Jacob waited to see if a few more ax blows might be needed. Then a certain movement of the huge trunk and more dry, tearing sounds sent Jacob leaping ten feet to the ground.

The top was wavering. Then the trunk leaned at an angle and started down—twisting, tearing at the still uncut fibers. There was a whistling high above, a prolonged swish, and the great weight descended, with the top arcing down and scraping against a smaller redwood at the edge of the clearing, stripping the bark as it crunched the wood. A hundred tons of fury struck the earth with an explosion that sent the pines and oaks hurtling up in a cloud of dust and cones. The mammoth redwood trunk bounced high, filling the air with flying branches and echoes of sound which continued to reverberate long after the log came to rest.

Then there was silence. And the silence seemed just as loud to Jacob Harlan's ears as had the crash of the falling tree. He brought his hands away from his ears, and was unable to speak. His tall companion, Dick Swift, stood staring, while Wiley Duff leaned on his ax, his jaws agitating a wad of tobacco. Finally Dick Swift found his tongue.

"Great smothering snakes! Did you ever see the likes of that, Jake?"

Jacob was still unable to answer. This was the most violent climax of his young life, yet he could not feel the elation, the excitement he had looked forward to. Instead his sensitive mind was burdened with the thought that by his hands and those of his companions one of the oldest living things on the earth had been killed. They had ended the life of a tree almost three thousand years old—a redwood that already had a sturdy, sound growth when the Romans were raiding Carthage.

Jacob Harlan realized also that his party was one of the first to bring down a California redwood—and that surely there would be many more cut down by many more men. There were an untold number of redwood trees in this new land, and with the people pouring in from the Eastern states there would be a growing need for lumber.

His own reason for going into the forest and attempting a task which most men considered too difficult had been simply the need for work and food. After leaving home he had found a welcome at his uncle's homestead in Mission San Jose but he needed to work and work was not easy to get. What work there was here in the San Francisco Bay area paid only eight or ten dollars a month. The few settlers around the Bay and the three hundred tent dwellers on the sandhills of Yerba Buena, now called San Francisco, were as poor as he was.

As Jacob walked from one settlement to another he found the big redwoods everywhere. They were magnificent trees, resembling the Western red cedar. Growing in clusters of ten to fifteen, the biggest ones were twenty feet in diameter or more, and two hundred feet high. The Latin name, he found, was *Sequoia sempervirens*.

The wood itself had fine qualities of endurance. It contained no pitch and did not catch fire as most other woods did. No insects would eat it and neither water nor sunshine would cause it to swell or shrink.

When the Spaniards were settling the area, they had cut

down and worked up a few trees, and at the Russian post, Fort Ross, the colonists had built blockhouses and palisades of the huge logs—warehouses, barracks, and chapels of the sawed boards. They had even sent thousands of cords by barge to the second Russian colony on the Farallon Islands. Along one or two rivers small camps of white men were whipsawing redwood and oak and there was a small sawmill on Los Gatos Creek.

This kind of backbreaking labor seemed the only answer to Jacob Harlan's problem. He was forced to the realization that to make a living he would have to cut down one of the great trees and split the wood into shingles for the roofs every cabin and house needed. Making a friend of Richard Swift, he hired him on the promise of wages to be paid when the shingles were cut and sold. With tools forged on the Harlan homestead and a poor thing of a crosscut saw borrowed from Jacob's uncle, the two boys set off for the Piedmont Hills east of San Francisco Bay.

They picked a redwood which would be most likely to fall cleanly into an open area where it could be cut conveniently and hand-split into shingles. They built the scaffold and boldly attacked the foot-thick bark. Then came the long, tedious, muscle-straining hours of wielding the broadax.

Weary and discouraged after a week's toil which seemed to show so little progress, Richard Swift dropped to the ground in exhaustion. When he managed to get on his feet he spoke the words Jacob had feared from the start.

"This is work for a dolt—somebody with strong arms and the sense of a goat. I'm going back to farming!"

Jacob kept chipping away with the ax, making no comment, and without further word his friend began sharpening his own blade. The work went on and at nightfall the boys had a visitor. The firelight showed them a man astride a saddle horse.

"How do, boys. Looks like ye set yerself a job. What in tarnation ye cuttin' a tree for? Or has a big beaver got loose on it? Plain to see yer no hands at it. Like as not I'll be fool enough to stay close on and see that big red feller come crackin' down."

Wiley Duff stayed on and was promised half the tree as his share in trade for his labor. Except for one day spent in shooting a deer and butchering it, he worked tirelessly, giving two strong arms to the saw and ax, and coloring his work with many humorous tales of his own exploits.

Then the momentous day came when the mammoth bulk lay on the ground and the task of making it into shingles began. In falling, the brittle redwood had broken into three pieces, the center section splitting.

"That will be yours, Wiley," Jacob announced. "How would it be if we helped you work it up? Then you can ride to San Antonio Landing and get us a wagon."

"Fine as flax, son," the mountaineer agreed. "But I'll do better. I'll ride in now and get more tools. We'll need a frow, a maul, and better axes. I'll borry what I kin. I'm aimin' to cut my share into mine timbers."

When he returned with tools, the timbers were chopped out, and he departed with the promise that he would sell them sight unseen and have the buyer come and get them. The boys began splitting shingles and in a week fifteen thousand were hauled to Bayside, then sent by flatboat to San Francisco where they were sold to a contractor, W. A. Leidsdorf. He paid Jacob Harlan five dollars a thousand, and Jacob gave Richard Swift half.

"You two are industrious boys," Leidsdorf told them. "How would you like to fence in some lots? Commodore Sloat, Mr. Stockton, and Colonel Fremont and others have over sixteen hundred vara lots here and they want to have fences built around them to keep the squatters out."

Jacob signed the contract to furnish mortised posts and rails for the lots. He and Dick Swift hired David Williamson in San Jose, set up a tent on Market Street, and once more took off for camp to split the redwood. Jacob also bought two yoke of oxen and a wagon, hiring his cousin Joel to do the hauling. When the contract was finished, all parties were satisfied and the young logger had five hundred dollars to divide among the four workers. It was more money than he had ever seen before.

Now the word was ringing through the forests that there was a market for redwood in San Francisco, and enterprising men followed the example of Jacob Wright Harlan. While he went on to other fields, the redwoods from Monterey to Mendocino began to fall and an industry was on its way to glory.

II

California . . . 1850

THE BIG FOUR OF MENDOCINO

GOLDEN GATE! Safe harbor after weary voyages around Cape Horn. San Francisco! Mecca of the gold seekers—romance, adventure, fortunes to be made.

In the fall of 1850 a certain four men looked around at the sprawling, brawling colony of tents and lean-tos, which at first was called Yerba Buena and later San Francisco. They wandered in and out of the flimsy board-and-canvas saloons, boardinghouses, and stores. They studied their fellow adventurers—a motley lot, ranging from bearded and unkempt teamsters and seamen to merchants and dandified gamblers.

San Francisco was a rawboned boom camp, the like of which might never be viewed again, but the four men saw little romance and adventure in it. They were looking for fortunes and they were not afraid to work hard for them. Yet now they wondered if they had not made a common mistake in coming here to this noisy clutter of broken dreams.

Mutual discouragement had brought them together. Edwards C. Williams had been a lieutenant in the First New York Volunteers during the war with Mexico, had come to San Francisco and set up a small lumberyard. He had found lumber easy to sell but hard to get. Harry Meiggs was a business opportunist, ready to turn his hand to any venture that promised quick reward. He had ample funds and good bank credit. Jerome Ford had tried his luck at gold mining and decided he wanted none of that life. Captain David Lansing had deserted the sea for whatever solid land could offer.

On this foggy evening in 1850 a cattle barge was towed in to the small wharf below Ed Williams' lumberyard. When he saw it was loaded with lumber and not steers, he was interested.

"Where does this come from?" he asked the barge tender.

"Bodega Bay," the man drawled. "Feller name of Smith—Cap'n Smith—got a sawmill up there in the big trees."

Williams bought the lot of unevenly sawed lumber and noticed that what it lacked in quality of board it made up for in its beautiful dark red color. He questioned the bargeman and learned the exact location of Captain Smith's sawmill.

"This is redwood," he told Harry Meiggs. "There are untold millions of feet of it all around here. Harry, the trees are immense—unbelievably big. In fact they are so big I doubt if there is anybody out here that would have the nerve or knowledge to cut them down and saw them up."

Anything was possible to Harry Meiggs. "This man Smith must have the nerve and knowledge," he said.

Williams acknowledged the fact and went on to describe the great redwood trees. No one who had not seen them would believe that trees could grow to such a size.

"Why Harry, some of those redwoods are so big twenty men with arms outstretched couldn't reach around them. They're the oldest living things on earth—the biggest ones three thousand years old. Think of it—over a thousand years old when Jesus was born."

Harry Meiggs nodded enthusiastically. "I know those trees, Ed, but until you came along with a spark in your eye I never thought much about making money on them. Do you think we could? How about it, Jerry? You— Captain Lansing?"

All four men agreed that with the "gold rush" still on, and all manner of ships bringing new people and money to the Bay area, San Francisco was bound to grow fast. This would mean building lumber could not be supplied fast enough.

Yes, the four men said, there was a great chance to make money in redwood and they set about organizing a company to buy the timber, cut and sell it. This enterprise was to be the first large-scale redwood lumbering operation in the fledgling state of California. The men pooled their money and credit. Edwards Williams was sent to Bodega Bay to survey the timber and see Captain Stephen Smith's mill. The great redwood trees were every bit as large and productive-looking as he expected but the sawmill was a small, portable affair, inadequate for handling the large quantities of timber envisioned by the new company. And Captain Smith was not too eager to talk business.

"Mr. Williams," he said, "if your party wants to go into this redwood business first class, you better go up the coast seventy or eighty miles and see what redwood forests are really like. There are more trees to one acre in Mendocino County than in ten here."

When Ed Williams reported this information to Harry Meiggs, it was at once decided Williams would have to go East, by ship through the Panama Canal, and buy proper sawmill machinery. In Connecticut, Williams came up against certain stumbling blocks and was in a quandary how to proceed without waiting months for an exchange of mail with his partner Meiggs. Then with great joy he discovered the telegraph had been invented during the four years he had been away from New York. Now in two days his problem was solved by telegrams to and from San Francisco.

He returned to that city as quickly as he could to find his three associates gone. He learned they had talked with a German settler named William Kasten who confirmed the existence of immense tracts of noble redwoods in the Mendocino area. They had at once chartered a small schooner, with Captain Lansing in charge, and sailed north. Now Edwards Williams received a message from Jerome Ford on the ship, saying that gales had forced the party into Bodega Bay. Williams lost no time in joining the other men there. Meiggs returned to San Francisco.

When the winds subsided the schooner sailed out to sea and made the wide mouth of Big River safely. This was a poor harbor, however, merely a pocket inside big rocks, which the sailors called a "dog hole." The schooner was anchored as securely as possible, the men praying that further gales would hold off and that tides would not be too strong. Leaving Captain Lansing and the crew aboard, Jerry Ford and Edwards Williams went upriver to prospect. Williams' written report to his partner Meiggs told of the trip.

> In a rough canoe, which he had fashioned from a redwood log, Mr. Ford and myself started out on a bright April morning with a fair light breeze from the ocean and a flood tide to prospect the river for timber. For the first half-hour we were rather disappointed, but after that all that we had hoped for was more than realized.
>
> The winter rains had not wholly ceased and the river banks were full, the slight ripples meeting the verdure of the shore, the tall redwoods with their great symmetrical trunks traveling towards the skies; with the bright colors of the rhododendrons profusely scattered over the hills forming the background, the clear blue sky above reflected in the placid river and over all the hush and solitude of the primeval forest —all combining to impress upon our minds the beauty and truth of the poetical line—"The groves were God's first temples"—and as I recall the beauty of the picture, I cannot but regret the part it appeared necessary for me to enact in what now looks like a desecration.
>
> Our dugout was a heavy awkward thing to handle and I think we had gone up the river not more than three and a half miles when on the first ebb tide we began to paddle homeward. This was a very different thing than our earlier experience. With wind and

tide setting forth our way, we had but little difficulty in going up, but on reversing our course we had a strong tide running out, helped by the accumulated fresh water which the flood tide had kept back, and as we approached the coast, the wind which was blowing up the river created a swell which threatened to fill and swamp our canoe with its scant two inches of freeboard. About one and a half miles from the ocean (as we judged) we tied up the canoe to the shore and started straight up the hill on the north side of the stream. After some scratched faces and bruised knees and shins we reached the top of the ridge and soon found a well-worn Indian trail which led westward, and before very long, saw the ocean again much to our joy. We had seen enough to satisfy us and the next morning with a fair wind, sailed for San Francisco, where we arrived without further misadventure.

The Bay was full of vessels now, many stranded because their crews had deserted to go to the mines and no new men wanted to ship out. By the time the sawmill machinery arrived from New England, the redwood party had bought one of these ships for little money—a six-hundred-ton brig named the *Ontario*. They loaded the new equipment on her, hired forty mechanics and laborers from the ranks of disgruntled and desperate miners, and once more set sail through Golden Gate.

The *Ontario* entered the broad Pacific and Captain Lansing soon discovered the ship had not been too much of a bargain after all. Having been anchored in San

Francisco Bay for such a long time, her planking above
the water line had dried out. Now, under the force of
wind and sea, the seams opened and leaks grew bigger
each day. Rounding Point Arena, the ship started taking
on water so fast that the men hired to build the sawmill
were put on pay to man the pumps constantly. Fortu-
nately no strong winds were encountered and the *Ontario*
sailed into Big River without accident.

Jerome Ford had been left in the city. He was to go
to Captain Stephen Smith's mill at Bodega, buying logging animals on the way, and then proceed overland to
Big River. His trip was beset by all the troubles man and
beast might expect to encounter going through an un-
tracked forest. He had taken the boat to Benecia, the
stage to Napa and Sonoma. There he hired two saddle
horses and a pair of pack mules, and witnessed a gun fight
between two miners from the Tuolumne, one of whom
shot out the other's teeth but did not kill him. Riding
to Bodega Corners, he stayed long enough with Captain
Smith to buy eight yoke of oxen and hire two drivers
for them.

The little cavalcade started out slowly and awkwardly,
crossed the South Fork of the Gualala River, and camped
that night. There were no roads, no trails except a few
tracks made by deer and elk. The rivers were at spring
flood and the only way to cross them was by swimming
the animals through the wide reaches of water. In the
raging waters of the Gualala, the mules broke loose and
drifted downstream. One of them drowned and the other,
unseating the driver and breaking back to shore, ran free
into the timber.

Jerry Ford and the second teamster got the bulls across the river and the man who had been tossed in managed to swim across. But all the provisions and blankets were gone with the mules and the party faced starvation with only saddle blankets, called "sweat cloths," to sleep under.

At an aggravating snail's pace the party tramped and stumbled on northward and after three miserable days came to what Jerry Ford called the "Portuguese Ranch." It was salvation and the men ate everything the kind rancher gave them. Replenishing stores the next day they followed down the Navarro River and then struck north again across the headwaters of the Big Salmon and Albion Rivers, gratefully staggering into a camp at the mouth of Big River, which the Indians called "Booldam," meaning "large stream."

Immediately Jerome Ford found that the brig *Ontario* had not yet arrived. The men were kept busy putting up semipermanent living quarters, getting the oxen shod for logging, and hiring some Indians to split rails for a bull corral. They got meat enough for a few days by killing an elk, and sent a party of three men to Little River where there was a trading post. Jerry Ford spent long evenings sitting on the point of land on the north bank of the river, looking out to sea for a speck of sail. His hope had just about turned to despair when the full spread of sail on the brig came into view.

Captain David Lansing worked the *Ontario* as close inshore as he dared. The cliffs rose seventy feet or more on both sides of the river and the tide boiled in menacingly. Only by skillful maneuvering could the ship's stern be brought close enough to land men and cargo. After two anxious days all equipment was ashore.

Then all hands were called to the task of blasting rocks and dirt off the cliffs to fill the brig's hold until her hull was resting on the bottom. The plan was to keep on filling her with rock, even between decks, to make of her a permanent wharf and breakwater. However the work was too long in the doing. A storm roared up, wind and waves came crashing down on the *Ontario*, breaking her upper works away from the anchored hull, and smashing the ship against the beach rocks. Even the weighted bottom was ripped loose and sent crashing into the breakers.

Now the work of building the sawmill and logging the big trees began. While the choppers sent their double-bitted axes ringing into the foot-thick red bark of trees twenty feet in diameter, men were sinking foundation piles for the mill. The first big tree crashed to earth and, with no cushioning for the tremendous weight, split and splintered into unusable tinder. The second tree, finally cut after seven days of chopping and sawing by two men, was made to fall on a bed of branches salvaged from the first tree. It came down intact. The trunk was cut into ten-foot sections, which the bull teams hauled to the river, and they floated down to the mill.

And the mill was meeting perplexing difficulties. The millwright, whom Williams had hired, was found to know little about the operation. Workmen became dissatisfied and deserted their jobs. Word was sent to Harry Meiggs in San Francisco, and he dispatched a new crew overland by the route Jerome Ford had taken.

Then winter storms set in and before the mill had its

roof on, the building was blown apart by gales. A nightmare of troubles beset every operation, but with dogged determination Edwards Williams had the mill completed and running by April—a full year after his return from the East Coast.

Within a month fifty thousand feet of lumber were coming out of the mill. The logging crew had been doubled and four more bulls had been imported. Harry Meiggs, still in San Francisco, was selling all the redwood he received, and was demanding more every month. Production was continually increasing and the company was incorporated as the Redwood Manufacturing Company, although it was still known by its original name—Mendocino Saw Mills.

It was lumber from this first big redwood operation, developed by Mendocino's "Big Four," which helped rebuild San Francisco after its first fires during the 1850's. It was the first redwood enterprise to use railroad track, over which oxen pulled lumber trucks from mill to loading chute on the high cliff, from where it was dropped to schooner decks. It was lumber from this pioneer mill which provided the first cargoes for the little two-masted schooners that dared enter the dog holes. The Big Four of Mendocino started a lumbering movement that became one of the important factors in the building of the West.

III

Oregon . . . 1850

SEA LEGS ASHORE

Asa Simpson was not happy about the present his father gave him on his tenth birthday. It was nothing he could eat, ride, or dig with, and it would be of no use to him until he was twenty-one. What a gift! A one thirty-second interest in whatever ship was a-building in the Simpsons' home town of Brunswick, Maine, when Asa became of age, seemed a sorry birthday surprise. The boy did not want his father to think him ungrateful but after his thank-you he said:

"But Dad, what if I study to be a doctor?"

"Well," his father answered with a dry chuckle, "maybe you'll be the ship's doctor. If not, and you don't go to sea, you'll at least have an investment."

And as it turned out on February 21, 1847, Asa M. Simpson had both—an investment consisting of a one thirty-second interest in the four-masted bark *Birmingham*, on the ways in Brunswick, and a desire to go to sea instead of being a doctor. By this time he also had a trade as a skilled shipbuilder. Two years later, his seagoing desire had kindled into a fever which had struck many other State of Mainers—the California gold fever.

Asa was twenty-three when he shipped as supercargo on the *Birmingham,* bound for Cape Horn; Valparaiso, Chile; and then Golden Gate. And he had begun a fabulous career as shipbuilder and shipmaster, lumbering pioneer on the Oregon and Washington coasts, and one of the great factors in Western timber manufacturing and shipping.

The *Birmingham* clewed up her sails in the harbor of San Francisco on April 7, 1850. Asa rowed ashore with the crew to find a city of tents and shacks sprawled over the sand hills. The harbor was filled with schooners and barges and full-rigged ships from England, China, and the seven seas—all of which had brought goods and gold seekers. Ringing the yerba buena bushes to the south, the west, and across the Bay to the Piedmont Hills were redwood forests, still beyond any dream of conversion to lumber. Up the Sacramento River lay more sand hills, Sutter's Mill, and the lure of gold.

The glitter of the yellow grains was in Asa Simpson's eye, too, but he had learned that a man makes a poor jump standing on one leg. He had to have money to get to the good digging and more money for tools and a grubstake. By exercising Yankee patience, helping to sell the *Birmingham*'s cargo so he could claim his share, he eventually got what he wanted.

While waiting, he built a small sailing skiff and located three men willing to pay their passage to Stockton where all four would go to the mines. Asa sailed the boat skillfully up the Sacramento River and his quest for gold began. It ended almost as quickly. The dirt and raw living, the close contact with hard drinkers, gamblers, and other unsavory characters cooled Asa's ardor. With hard work and considerable luck he had panned out fifteen hundred dollars at the end of three weeks and had the good sense to stay away from the snares of three-card monte and the poker tables.

Like many other gold seekers he soon learned that for every man who struck it rich in the mines, a hundred lost everything. Equally important was his observation that the wise man made his money by furnishing services to the foolhardy fortune seekers. Accordingly he saw opportunity while crossing the Bay into San Francisco—the bare ribs of a ship on the ways. She was a steamer.

"What's her name to be?" he asked the foreman of the job the next day.

"The *H. T. Clay.*"

"That's a grand name. Looks like a pretty little craft. Good lines. You know your business, mister. I'm a shipbuilder myself. Simpson's my name—Asa M. Simpson from Brunswick, Maine."

They shook hands. "Glad to know you, young Simpson. Shipbuilder, eh? I'm Tod Beasley from Bedford, Mass. Want to go to work, Mr. Simpson? Take off your coat. Here's a broadax. Start trimming up those knees."

This was the start of Asa's second financial venture, and the first of his many disasters. In later years he was to look back on all the ships lost and all the sawmills burned to the ground and weigh these tragedies against his successes.

"I guess I spent my whole life getting knocked down and getting up again," he said.

He sank his fifteen hundred dollars into the building

ABOVE: Grove of California redwood trees, still alive after 3000 years. RIGHT: Three days' chopping had only chipped away three feet of the great bulk. *(Page 17)*.

Curtis Annand

ABOVE: "Twenty men with arms outstretched couldn't reach
around them." *(Page 22).* BELOW: Port Gamble mill was the
largest producer of fir in the world for forty years. *(Page 46).*

Jesse E. Ebert Collection

of the *H. T. Clay* to carry passengers to Sacramento or Stockton for one ounce of gold. But dozens of ships began arriving from the East Coast and other ports to compete with the *H. T. Clay* in getting passengers. Fares dropped to $5 and freight to 12 cents a hundred pounds. The venture was a costly loss.

Dejectedly Asa Simpson—a hardened businessman at twenty-four—wandered along the waterfront looking for work and encouragement. For many days he wished he were back home and then he realized such a return would mean admitting he had failed. And failure was a word he did not like.

He knew nothing about lumber—had no "wood sense," as he called it. But he did have business sense and when his endless wanderings took him back to the bark *Birmingham*, he saw that the lumber she had brought was still piled on the wharf. He owned a thirty-second share of this and he literally pounced on it, selling it all in a few days to a man going to the gold fields. The proceeds paid some of Asa's debts and bought him a third interest in the schooner *Potomac*. This gave him a steady berth for several months and when the vessel sailed for the Columbia River and Portland the following spring, 1851, her holds full of sugar, clothing, machinery, and general merchandise, Asa was signed on as mate.

The *Potomac*'s voyage north was a shipmaster's dream, fair winds speeding her up along the coast. On the day watches Asa could catch glimpses of great forests lining the shore, ranging from the redwoods in California to fir and spruce in Oregon. On the lonely night watches he wondered how the trees could be cut and the lumber sold.

Then suddenly the *Potomac's* luck ran out. The Columbia River bar was already a graveyard of bigger and finer ships and the shrieking gales had even less mercy on a little schooner like the *Potomac*. The storm blew her on a sand spit like a chip on a lake, swept her sails and deck load into the breakers, and hammered her hull for forty-eight hours. Then Providence intervened. The gale abated and out from Astoria came the steamer *Lot Whitcomb,* commanded by Captain Joseph Kellogg. She towed the *Potomac* off the spit and on up the Columbia to the settlement of Portland.

There was literally nothing but forests at this pioneer port where the Willamette River flowed into the Columbia. And with the *Potomac* repaired, Asa M. Simpson loaded her with lumber and piling, and had Captain Kellogg tow her downriver to Astoria. There was much activity in this town, born of the fur trading of John Jacob Astor, and again there were untold millions of feet of lumber still to be cut out of the thousands of acres of virgin timber—Douglas fir, Sitka spruce, and Western red cedar. But Asa, thinking he was a seafaring man first, set sail for San Francisco with his first command.

However, wood had already begun to mix with salt water in the Simpson veins and the next year saw Captain Asa back in Astoria building a small sawmill. The venture was ill-starred. With poor advice and green labor the mill was "just the kind," people said, "a sea captain who knows nothing about sawmills would build." It turned out to be another costly failure and Captain Asa went back to sea in the schooner *Harriet,* sailing her down the Oregon coast to the Umpqua River.

Here he found a crew cutting piling and his vessel was engaged to transport the lumber to San Francisco. "But you'll have to wait a month or more," the piling contractor told him, "before we can cut a whole shipload. Why don't you sail up the river to Scottsburg?"

"I may be a crazy shipmaster," Captain Asa replied, "but not crazy enough to sail up a river with variable winds or none against a current, and with Indians on both banks ready to salvage a grounded vessel and murder us all.

"No," he continued with a hard gleam in his blue eyes, "I think I'll take my mate and a husky seaman and walk down the beach to what is called Coos Bay. The Indians around here say it's 'one sun long sand.' Know anything about it?"

The timber cutter scowled. "I wouldn't believe anything an Indian said. Go talk to General Hooker at the government station at Gardiner."

The Simpson party did this and the General advised against any beach hike. There were a lot of Indians, he said, and they were savage. In spite of his advice, Asa and the two sailors started off down the coast. At Ten Mile Creek, which was wide, shallow, and swift, they saw Indians on the opposite bank and decided the Army man had been right, since these Rogue River braves wore paint, plumes, and feathers, had their faces tattooed, and looked anything but friendly.

The voyagers returned to the Umpqua, sailing the *Harriet* loaded with piling to San Francisco. But young Captain Simpson—he was twenty-nine then—felt a drive to return to the Oregon coast and its magnificent timber resources. He went back to the Umpqua and again went beach walking. This time he did get to Coos Bay and there he stayed at Empire City which was to mean both reward and tragedy.

News traveled slowly in the vast timber-bound area and when trappers shuffled into the little store to meet fishermen and exchange gossip, one subject was the sudden appearance of piles driven at the edge of the deep-water bay, for not one sawmill but two.

"That's right, pardner—two sawmills. One is Mr. Henry Luse's—him that got free land from Captain Billy Harris who got it free from the gov'mint and built a cabin and laid out the town, all eight blocks of it and called it Empire 'cause that's the biggest thing he could think of. Well, no, I don't know yet who's puttin' up the other mill. Some daffy feller from San Francisco, most likely."

The "daffy feller" was Captain Simpson, making his second venture into sawmilling. He had struck up a friendship with Henry Luse and Captain William H. Harris, bought 160 acres of tideland for three hundred dollars, and started the underpinning of a mill. Henry Luse was just as intelligent and energetic and had already brought in sawmill machinery. Now there was a race on to see which man would be sawing first in the new steam plants.

By this time Asa's two brothers, Louis and Robert W., had come West and the three met in San Francisco. Asa and Louis bought the machinery that had been used in gold pioneer John Sutter's mill—an old-fashioned "Down East" sash saw—loaded it with other necessities on the coasting schooner *Quadratus,* skippered by a Captain Butler, and sailed north.

The Coos Bay bar had always been a treacherous stretch of water—a mile-long reef passable only on full tides and beset by capricious winds which made the crossing doubly hazardous for sailing ships. But the *Quadratus,* argued the headstrong Butler, was a sturdy vessel and he a skillful sailing master. If anybody could take the schooner into Coos Bay, he was the man. There was scant wind when the vessel edged up to the bar and both Asa and Louis Simpson advised the master to keep sounding constantly and not try to cross until he was sure he had full tide.

"How many people does it take to run my ship!" stormed Captain Butler. "Cap'n Simpson, eh? Maybe you was captain in the horse marines. Tide's flooding now and this little sou'wester breeze'll float us right over."

Without Butler's knowledge Captain Asa had dropped his own sounding lead on the starboard side and the reading was nine fathoms—then seven, and six. He appealed to the master to swing to the north, telling him the tide was ebbing and that the ship would surely founder.

With the skipper's ridiculing answer came a grinding crash. The *Quadratus* went over on her beam ends, the deck load of machinery breaking away from its lashings and sweeping two seamen and Louis Simpson into the frothy breakers. As the hull planks gave way and the vessel filled, Asa saw his brother's crushed body floating over the crests, then passing out of sight. The seas broke over him as he knelt and prayed for strength and forgiveness of Captain Butler.

This blow was the mightiest yet in Asa Simpson's life and could well have smothered a weaker man. He had not only lost a brother who had great promise and would have been a valuable asset in the new steam sawmill enterprise but he had lost most of the mill machinery.

The *Quadratus* was heeled full over and the waves were getting higher with the increasing force of the wind. But miraculously the ship stirred and her masts seemed to lift off the water. Sure enough she was righting herself and both seamen knew the tide had changed. The schooner had struck the bar at the extreme low and now was free of the bottom. As she gathered seaway the sails filled once more and the helmsman had her pointed into Coos Bay. She gained the harbor and then as Captain Asa's eye made out the building on shore which had been erected while he was away, billows of black smoke rose from it. This was salt in his wounds. Henry Luse was sawing.

The first thing Asa Simpson did on getting ashore was to congratulate his rival, and Henry Luse in turn was shocked to learn of the tragedy on the bar. A friendship developed, although the two remained business competitors.

"Look here, Asa," Luse said. "I'm cutting eight to ten thousand feet of lumber a day. Why don't you fill up that ship of Butler's and take it to Frisco. You can make more money shipping and selling lumber than you can trying to cut it. You have no mill machinery and can't complete your building . . ."

"Now hold on, Henry," Asa interrupted. "I didn't lose all my machinery—nothing I can't replace. The sawing machine, yes—and some pulleys and gears. But the boiler's intact. Mark you—I'll finish the mill. But first, I'll buy enough lumber from you to build a shipyard."

"A shipyard!" Luse exclaimed. "That's just what I was going to do."

"Fine, fine," said Asa. "We'll see who can build the most and the best. You and I were meant to challenge each other. I'll wager you right now, I'll turn out the first ship."

That was one wager he won. While his sawmill was being finished, Asa built a lumber schooner almost before Henry Luse could get started. Both yards were successful. During the 1860's they launched fifty-eight vessels. One of them, the *Western Shore,* was the first full-rigged ship built on the Pacific Coast. The port of Empire became the Coos County seat with a customhouse. And the Simpson mill prospered. The fine Port Orford cedar, which grew only in a small belt along the coast, brought a premium price in San Francisco for shipbuilding and for manufacture into lucifer matches, broom handles, lath and barrel staves.

In 1857, after his brother Captain Robert W. came from San Francisco to join him, Asa's enterprises included a packet line of five vessels between San Francisco and Portland—the *Tam O'Shanter, Webfoot, Melancthon, Whistler,* and *Portland*—all familiar sights along the coast. A steam tug service was started, in connection with Captain George Flavel, to help ships across the Coos Bay bar.

Then disaster struck the Port Orford operation, when flames swept through the timber, destroying the pioneer mill, all logs, lumber, homes, stable, office, and tools. The loss was so complete that Captain Asa gave the land and ruins to his old friend Joseph Nay. Seeking new territories to conquer, he went back to the Umpqua River and built the first sawmill there—on the A. C. Gibbs claim—at a point called Gardiner. This mill also burned but the great trees surrounding it were spared, so a new building was erected, and more modern machinery installed. A man named George H. Emerson was put in charge.

And again farther north, Asa Simpson returned to the country he had always loved, the Columbia River bank near Astoria. Men named Knapp and Grant had a sawmill there but it had not been a success. Asa bought it and made it one. The town of Knappton grew up around the mill.

Then he went farther north into the raw state of Washington. Tapping the greatest Douglas fir forest on the whole globe, Asa Simpson, with two Riddell brothers, built a mill on Willapa Harbor at a point called South Bend. A few years later he started the first mill on Grays Harbor at Hoquiam and brought George Emerson up from the Umpqua to run it.

Captain Asa M. Simpson had now proved to himself that a man could be knocked down and come up roaring —also that a sea captain could make a "right passable land lubber." He was a success but he had a long way still to travel. He had more setbacks with the Empire mill —one fire after another. When the most crippling one struck in 1885, he bought out his brother Robert's interests and changed the name of the enterprise to the Simpson Lumber Company, making his young son, Louis J., its president. A second Coos Bay mill was acquired from the California Lumber Company. All this was the foundation for the new town of North Bend, which has since become famous in lumber production and shipping.

When Captain Simpson retired to live in San Francisco, his many lumber activities passed into the hands of younger men, his name and energies an inspiration to them. In a later day Asa wandered down to the Montgomery Street wharves where the steam schooner *A. M. Simpson* was unloading fir poles from her decks. He saw two men talking and listened to the conversation.

"A. M. Simpson," one said. "I knew him—a rock transplanted from Maine—and a great man I'll tell you. He took some awful beatings but always came back for more. I know for a fact he lost over twenty ships—and not a one insured."

"I knew him too," the other said. "He was a seaman of the first water and his legs went ashore. Yes, he was great —he never let those legs take root."

Asa Simpson chuckled in his beard and walked on.

IV

Washington . . . 1853

TREASURE IN TREES

"GREAT jumping Jupiter—just look at that timber!"

The man at the helm had forgotten for a moment his Yankee reserve and caution. He had come to this country expecting to find trees and start a sawmill but what he saw now was almost beyond belief.

After his first sight of the timber, he worked the ship inshore for closer inspection. For miles along the coastline, which was the northern shore of the Olympic Peninsula on the Strait of Juan de Fuca, the forest extended in a solid, unbroken line. As deep as the eye could penetrate, the spire-topped trees extended back, to touch the flanks of the mountains' snow ridges. Here was land so densely wooded it seemed to the ship's captain to be the enchanted forest of a fairy tale.

Yet Captain William C. Talbot was a practical man— imaginative, but not a dreamer. He was, in a sense, as much an explorer in these lands as Captains Cooke and Vancouver had been years before. But he had a mission. He was to meet another Maine expedition here and build a sawmill. And if there had ever been doubts in his mind about the quantity of timber to be cut, they were gone

now. There were millions and millions of feet of lumber
hidden under the bark of all those fir, cedar, and spruce
trees. What he had heard about the fir forests of Washington Territory was true. And he knew this would be
the end of his voyaging for a little while at least.

The little brig *Julius Pringle* bore down the Strait to
Discovery Bay and anchored. In this month of June,
1853, she was thirty days out of San Francisco, loaded
with tools, foodstuffs, trade goods for the Indians, and
some Maine pine for shelters and cookhouse while the
men were starting the sawmill. And now Captain Talbot
was wondering where in all this vast expanse of timber
would be the best place to build it.

He launched two boats, manning the sailing skiff himself and putting Cyrus Walker and millwright E. S. Brown
in the canoe. They worked down into Puget Sound, saw
the little sawmill of W. P. Sayward being built in Admiralty Inlet, and J. J. Felt's mill at Apple Tree Cove which
was already cutting logs. They explored Hood Canal and
were attracted to a sheltered bay with a level, sandy spit
at one side—a place the Indians called Teekalet. The
Talbot party took soundings and cruised the timber which
seemed endless. The fir and spruce trees ranged from tall,
slender shafts, which would be ideal for ship spars and
piling, to giant boles eight and ten feet in diameter, which
would produce fine clear boards and timbers. The cedar
would make excellent shingles and weatherboards.

"We'll build the mill here," said Captain Talbot.

Those five words signaled the beginning of the great
Pope and Talbot enterprises. For over forty years its Puget
Sound sawmills were the largest producers of fir in the

world—lumber which helped build and rebuild San Francisco, Hawaii, and Australia. The empire controlled a fleet of ships and tugs and sawmills on Grays Harbor and in Oregon, and its holdings included many thousands of feet of timber and land.

The *Julius Pringle* was unloaded, a crew of men was left to sink the pilings for the mill and erect shelters, and the ship set sail for Seattle at the foot of Puget Sound.

In this small settlement, where a few hundred people were grouped in tents and cabins on the hillsides in back of a log post office, Captain Talbot shook hands with Henry Yesler who had just started a small steam sawmill on the waterfront and with Captain William Renton who was building one outside the bay at Alki Point. Henry Yesler laughed.

"So you came 'way out here from State of Maine to try to run me out of business. Go right ahead, captain. The more the merrier. This country will grow with our help."

"It is that," agreed William Talbot, "and I don't think we could run you out of business if we wanted to. There are four of us in the Puget Mill Company—Andrew Pope who is going to stay in San Francisco to sell our lumber, Charles Foster, myself, and Captain J. P. Keller, who is sailing out here with another party from East Machias, Maine, in the schooner *L. P. Foster*. They're due pretty soon. Our plan is to ship everything we cut out of the Sound to San Francisco and beyond. We'll have our own ships."

As the captain spoke, there was a look of such confidence in his gray eyes, that Yesler could see progress and success in the making. The *Pringle* returned to the mill site and Talbot found that his aides, Cyrus Walker and E. S. Brown, had visited the Indians across the bay. They could expect no trouble from them, the men said, and not much help either.

"They're Makahs and friendly. In fact they trust white men more than they do some other Indian tribes. A party of Haidas from the islands north of here raided their camp a little while ago and they've got half a dozen injured men in their slab houses."

"Will the men work for us?" Talbot asked.

Walker shook his head. "Not likely—and they'd not be trustworthy or steady. We traded them yard goods for fish, and went out with two bucks in one of their canoes, hollowed out of a cedar log. They're expert fishermen and these waters are alive with salmon—and halibut out in the Straits and ocean. The squaws smoke salmon and make baskets, too."

"Get the Makahs to work if you can. I brought a few men from Seattle and more will come later. Now Cyrus —Captain Keller and the *Foster* should be here any day but I can't wait. I must take the *Pringle* back to Frisco. I'll probably pass Keller on the high seas."

But his luck was better than that. The meeting was to be more dramatic. Captain Talbot hoisted sail and the brig had no sooner tacked into the westerly wind when a lookout shouted "Sail ho!" The two ships closed in, exchanged greetings, and then, from across the water, came the words:

"Schooner *L. P. Foster* out of Boston a hundred and fifty-four days for Puget Sound."

Shouts and whistles sounded from deck to deck as the

two vessels stood head on, riding the swells and chop as though jumping in excitement. Captain Talbot was rejoicing, as he passed the news of the mill site to Captain Keller and wished him well. Then the *Pringle* trimmed her sails again and charted her course out past Cape Flattery.

Captain Keller's timely arrival at the Port Gamble mill with engines, boilers, merchandise, and stores, workers and their wives, stepped up the pace of the sawmill building. The saw was a crude up-and-down "muley" but within a week it was turning out boards from the first small log, which were used to frame the mill and side it against rain and wind. During later months a sash saw was added as well as a gang saw into which a whole log could be fed and cut at once.

A new building was erected and more modern machinery installed so that logs eight and nine feet in diameter could be handled without having to blast them apart with a charge of powder. A carriage 125 feet long was constructed on which ship planking 60 feet long could be sawed and ship spars shaped. With production increasing steadily, schooners and barkentines began arriving. The tug *Resolute* was purchased to tow them in and out of the harbor.

One of these ships carried Captain W. C. Talbot, returning to Port Gamble. He loaded the *L. P. Foster* with piling and sailed at once for San Francisco where most of the cargoes went. A. J. Pope was stationed there permanently to dispose of the company's products.

In 1854 the *Ella Francis* took the first cargo to Australia. The French ship *St. Joseph* also carried Puget Mill lumber there and the company chartered the brig *Aeolian* to carry ship planking and spars to Hong Kong.

One foggy November morning in 1856, going outside his cabin for firewood, a millhand was startled by a knife flying into the woodpile and the sudden appearance of a squat, swarthy Indian, his black hair bound up in a red cloth. Expecting to be attacked, the man breathed easier when he saw the buck was trying to warn him about something. He understood enough of the Makah jargon to make out that more Indians were coming. The marauders were not Makahs from across the bay at Teekalet, but savage tribes from the northern islands of Queen Charlotte and Alexander.

The lone Makah disappeared as stealthily as he had come and the workman sounded the alarm through the camp. Captain Keller had built a two-story blockhouse, which he called "Malakoff," but it had never been used and had now fallen into disrepair. The few wives and children were herded into it while the mill whistle tooted frantically and the men attempted to plug up the gaps in the stockade walls, and store away rifles, powder, and provisions for a siege. Captain Keller took command with Cyrus Walker his ready aide.

As the mill people waited for the Indian raid, a scout reported a camp of warlike Indians across the bay. They had fallen upon the unsuspecting colony of Makahs, killed one or two who had resisted them, stolen women and food. Even as he gave the news smoke drifted in with the fog, and the crackle of fire and strident screams bounded across the bay.

In the face of this threat the mill continued idle, the

workers alert and waiting inside the blockhouse. During the night and the next morning, sounds of rifle shots and a cannon booming echoed through the woods. Toward noon a figure was seen in a creeping approach. The watchful guardians were all ready to shoot when they recognized the uniform of a U.S. Navy sailor. At once they lowered their guns and opened the gates.

"I'm from the warship *Massachusetts*," the sailor told the eager throng of settlers as he gratefully drank the coffee handed him. "She's here to put down this pesky Indian uprising. What started it was that gold discovery over east of the mountains around Fort Colville. The miners got those Yakimas and Spokanes all riled up so a couple of thousand of them came around and got these Puget Sound Indians mad too. They attacked Seattle, killed two young fellows, took cattle and stuff, and set fire to a lot of houses. The garrisons at Steilacoom and Vancouver got busy and sent the sloop-of-war *Decatur* up here to Puget Sound."

Captain Keller interrupted the seaman. "But these Indians on the warpath are tribes from islands to the north."

"Right, sir," the Navy man assured him, "and that's why we're here. Those Haidas are bad actors. Soon as these local Indians got stirred up, that bunch of heathens took advantage of it to come scooting south in their war canoes as fast as the wind and raise cane around here. We dropped some balls into their camp and sent in a landing party. One of our men—a friend of mine, too— Gus Englebrecht—was killed. Don't know what's going to happen now but those Indians can't do much with a warship on top of them."

The seaman was right. The uprising was put down by the *Massachusetts* after a few skirmishes, the Haidas surrendering and agreeing to go back to their homes. After burying the white casualty, the man-of-war sailed away.

The Puget Mill Company went to work again and with some feeling of insecurity maintained a guard on the sand spit. But the Indian scare brought them benefits instead of more trouble and delays. Many mill workers who had fled Seattle during the attack had come to Port Gamble to work. Among them were young men who were later to return to lead the town to prominent heights.

From the Pope and Talbot shipyards in East Machias, Maine, came a steady flow of ships for Puget Mill, as it was a stated policy for the company to own as many "bottoms" as it could, in order to control lumber shipments. By 1861 ten vessels flew the P.M. insignia and were on regular runs with lumber for San Francisco and Hawaii, bringing back coconut oils, fruit, and mixed cargo. These were the *Francisco, Constitution, Hyack, Jenny Ford, Kutusoff, Leonore, Oak Hill, Torrent, Vernon,* and *Victor.*

Less than ten years after landing on Puget Sound, Captain Keller died, ending the career of an intrepid shipmaster and lumber pioneer. Cyrus Walker then became the managing head of the sawmill and carried the company to fabulous success. The Civil War years, business recessions, and competition posed their problems but Puget Mill Company continued to expand and prosper. The company was a substantial influence in the economic life of Puget Sound cities, as the many Pope and Talbot enterprises grew into a world-wide empire.

V

California . . . 1870

DAREDEVIL OF THE DOG HOLES

WHEREVER else courage was shown in the early logging of the Western woods, it roared out like a lion on the little steam schooners that carried the redwood lumber from sawmills to San Francisco and the Sandwich Islands. It took all the qualities a man could muster, from ambition to endurance, to bring the giant trees to earth, and cut them into lengths that bull teams could haul to rivers or sawmills. It took the same qualities to build sawing machinery to handle the big logs. But vast bravery and raw courage characterized the masters of the small ships that dared to enter the "dog holes" of California's Mendocino coast.

There were not very many of these skippers, not nearly enough in fact. As lumber piled up at the little mills, their owners fumed and fussed, watching the horizon like eagles day after day, in the hope of seeing some ship working inshore. Most of the time ships did not come—for the simple reason that men did not dare to chance sudden death and the loss of their ships in the boiling pots of rock-bound anchorages. Captain "Midnight" Olsen was one who did dare. He took chances in the line of duty, no matter how dangerous they were. Once on a wharf in Arcata he said to a new mate who had just signed on for his first voyage to San Francisco:

"We should have good weather this trip. Ought to clear Golden Gate in twenty days. We'll go in ballast to Rockport and pick up cargo there. 'Course if one of those pesky sou'westers shows up, it might take thirty. No longer than that unless the wind whacks us while we're at anchor—then you could be seein' Frisco from the bottom of the cove. Well—I made every trip so far."

Before that voyage was over, the new mate had learned about Mendocino's dog holes and, like many other officers, turned his back on them, to ship out on barks and steamers for South Pacific seas which involved ordinary risks, leaving redwood cargoes for the brave and foolhardy.

Captain Olsen knew this coast. He had sailed it for years and the name on the ships' articles was Gudmund Olsen, Master. He was a Norwegian with a Viking's love for the sea and expectation of a watery grave. Whatever dangers his ship encountered were part of a seaman's life, and his job was to keep the ship afloat and the lives of his crew intact.

The name "Midnight" was as much a part of him as his lean, dour, rugged face. He earned it when he was skipper of the 416-ton *Acme,* a schooner out of Alameda, California. For years she maintained a regular run between the Humboldt Bay ports of Eureka and Arcata and San Francisco, carrying lumber, general cargo, and, most important, mail. There was no other means of transporting mail except by the uncertain stagecoaches and Captain Olsen felt his responsibility to the pioneer settlers along the coast. Three or four ships would approach the rough and treacherous Humboldt bar in the black of night and usually lie outside until daylight. But night was the same as day to Gudmund Olsen and the *Acme*. In fair weather, foul weather, or fog, she "hitched up her skirts" and rode in or out of Humboldt Bay, even when the tide allowed only a few inches of water under her keel. And so this skipper's name became Captain "Midnight" Olsen.

In the rivalry between coasters, the shipmasters would lay wagers to see which vessels would make the Humboldt Bay to San Francisco run in the fastest time. Midnight Olsen did not always win but he always tried. He raced the *San Pedro, Aberdeen,* and *Point Arena* and always had a better-than-average chance to be the first to finish the two-hundred-mile run by passing Alcatraz Island in San Francisco Bay. Only the worst weather or the heaviest cargoes delayed the *Acme*.

Once the little steamer caught a gale off Point Reyes and fought it like a tiger almost to Golden Gate. Then she fell off her course slightly and the sea mounted her decks and snatched away three thousand feet of her lumber deck load to smash it down on the deckhouse. But although heavily crippled, the *Acme* made port with all hands.

On another voyage the *Acme* fouled her rudder on the rocks off the Albion River. She was outward bound with a full cargo of redwood, and the sea had carried her against the rocks with such terrific force that the skipper thought the bottom might be damaged. The rudder operated to some extent but before he took his vessel out to deep water he would have to make an inspection. Since there was no other way to do it, Captain Midnight stripped off his clothes and went over the side into the paralyzingly cold water. He came up by the Jacob's ladder, reported no damage on the starboard side of the hull, warmed himself in the boiler room, and dived again. After three more submarine inspections he was satisfied the *Acme* could go to sea safely and she steamed south for San Francisco where the bent rudder shaft was repaired.

Some of the bravery and daring Captain Midnight Olsen displayed was due to the fact that he knew his ship and the places where she was going. As the *Acme* lay at moorage off Greenwood on one occasion, the barometer began falling and storm clouds formed off to the southwest. It was in the gale season of late October and the shipmaster knew trouble could be expected. He had some lumber in the *Acme*'s hold but for an hour now the wire chute had not been working—no more cargo was being sent down. Captain Olsen stood aft impatiently waiting for loading to start again.

It did—for just a few more boards. Then a message from the sawmill foreman said that waves were breaking over Gunderson Rock two miles out and it was dangerous to load more lumber. He warned that if the schooner didn't heave her anchors and ride out the storm beyond the dangerous shoal rocks, she would be battered to pieces. The captain's lusty answer was a challenge to the stormy gusts whipping out of the southwest.

"I don' get my sailin' orders from shore. By sixteen fouled up mizzen tops—me and this ship are here to get a cargo and if we don't get it some other sea cook will."

The *Acme* jerked at her anchor lines like a whale on a leash. Captain Midnight Olsen stood on her heaving deck and shouted in a voice that the gale batted to the men on the cliff:

"I'm less than half loaded! Send down more lumber!"

Some lumber came swaying down and more weather came whistling through the schooner's stays and guylines. The mill foreman saw unswerving determination in the doughty skipper's actions and gave in. The waves and swells mounted heavily as bundles of redwood shingles, lattice, and planks came rattling down the cable. Then the seas became vicious, the *Acme* danced, bounded, and pitched. She pulled at her anchor lines until those on shore thought surely the little vessel would come crashing on the rocky cliffs. Some on deck may have thought so too—even Captain Midnight himself. When the lumber stopped coming the second time, he broke out in wild protests and then, philosophically accepting the weakness and stubborn freakishness of land-bound sawmillers, gave his attention to the storm.

For twenty hours he used every tactic and trick of seamanship to keep the *Acme* from foundering. He shortened his chains and lengthened them, dropping a spare anchor for added security. The gale developed into a squall, with sudden twisting gusts, and the vessel was in a constant turmoil, a little chip in a boiling pot. Clouds broke overhead and drenched him with cold bullets of rain which gave him a double lacing as the wind sucked them back off the cliff. But he braced himself against the wheel house and took the *Acme*'s lurchings with all the rest of the furor. At dawn the ship was still there, staunchly defending her right to be there. The discouraged gale had passed northward, leaving only great ground swells. The mill men were satisfied that Captain Midnight knew his business and they sent down more cargo—only wishing they knew their business half so well.

The *Acme* was only one of half a hundred coastal ships that carried the redwood cargoes to market during the fifty years from 1865 to 1915. Captain Midnight Olsen commanded several ships besides the *Acme*—the *Whitesboro, Brunswick, Santa Monica, Coquille River, Elizabeth,* and *Samoa.* He had many hair-raising experiences and rarely did he reach port without getting news that one of his friends and fellows shipmasters had been lost at sea. He dreaded walking up Montgomery Street in San Francisco or Second Street in Eureka after a voyage and hearing that the *Melito* or some other ship had come to grief and her captain would no longer be able to yarn with him. He would rather take a ninety-mile-an-hour lashing off Point Arena than hear tidings like these.

His ship had just tied up at Field's Landing in July, 1907, when word was brought to him that Captain Peter Moran and the coastwise passenger steamer *Columbia* were now added to the casualties of the sea and would steam no more. As he learned the tragic details, he realized more and more that no matter how skillful a navigator a shipmaster was, "eternal vigilance is the price of liberty."

The *Columbia* had left San Francisco bound for Puget Sound with two hundred passengers and a crew of thirty-six. Off Cape Mendocino, the first night was very dark, the moon obscured by a heavy cloud bank, fog thickening and closing in on a flat sea.

The *Columbia* was steaming full ahead with Captain Moran pacing the bridge nervously. A ship's whistle sounded sharply off to starboard and at once a vessel's running lights appeared in the fog. The master's order to reverse engines was effected at once, but the *Columbia's* momentum continued to carry her forward. Whistles of both ships sounded frantically and then the sharp prow of the second vessel crushed into the *Columbia's* waist. Lifeboats were swung out and passengers swarmed into them but the steamer settled fast on her starboard beam, smothering boats and bodies. As she sank, Captain Moran was still on the bridge.

The ship that had rammed the steamer was the steam schooner *San Pedro,* loaded to her half-deck with redwood ties and timbers, which the collision flung in sprawling confusion. Her hull was also badly damaged and she was taking on water to a dangerous degree. She settled so low that water washed over the clutter on her deck, which now included a few of the *Columbia's* passengers who had been pulled from the sea. With only seventy of them, and a few rescued crewmen, the *San Pedro* reversed her course and headed back to Humboldt Bay. The *George W. Elder,* following the steamer lane just after the crash, rescued others floating helplessly in the sea.

Captain Midnight Olsen vividly remembered this disaster and others which were continually occurring in a day when ships were completely at the mercy of storms and fires in the holds, when the only chance of rescue was a passing ship sighting an inverted ensign on the mast or a barrel of pitch burning on the deck, and the only escape was by jumping into lifeboats if they could be launched.

Yet he continued his daring adventures into the rocky pockets of the coastline in the firm belief that a shipmaster kept going ahead until his time came. His had not come yet nor had there been any signs that it would come. So when he was told that there was a lumber cargo at Navarro, he steamed toward the headlands until he could see specks of buildings perched on the bluff.

The captain knew this anchorage and the method necessary to load his ship. The shallow dog hole was one of the worst on the whole Mendocino coast and the chute down which the lumber slid was notorious as a rickety contraption which looked as though it would sag or break in half and drop into the frothy surf at any moment.

The buildings Captain Olsen could see from his ship were lumber storage sheds. The sawmill was a mile upriver. The logs were hauled out of the gulch by bull teams and the lumber pulled up a crude tramway to the higher level where it was stored in the sheds. The chute extended downward about eighty feet at a forty-five-degree angle, the upper half of it over the rocks of the shore, the lower half, over the angry water, supported by a flimsy A-frame type of trestle. The extreme lower end of the chute was guyed to some steadiness by cables which ran up over the apex of the A and were anchored to spikes driven in the rocks.

The sea was rough as the schooner made a landfall. Captain Midnight noticed that the barometer was falling and knew well enough many skippers would not chance entering the shallow water inside the ring of rocks. But he could now see a white flag being run up as a signal that his ship had been sighted and that a cargo of lumber was ready. Captain Midnight meant to have it.

With a final calculation of wind and tide, he posted lookouts fore and aft, ordered half speed ahead. Handling the wheel himself, he pointed the five-hundred-ton schooner *Mayfair* toward the river mouth. "Slow" signaled the engine-room bell and he swung the bow to port, then sharply back to starboard and then to port again. Following waves lifted the schooner high and pushed her down into the troughs but under skillful handling she came back on course and slowly felt her way around and between the shoal rocks. She seemed almost to strike the shoreline but her skipper knew both ship and sea bottom, and maneuvered until the schooner stood out a hundred yards from the end of the spidery lumber chute. Then he put the *Mayfair* into a half circle and with utmost caution allowed her to drift shoreward to within fifty yards of the chute end. Then he sang out:

"Let go for'ard anchor! Give her twelve fathoms."

The hook plummeted and the chain came taut.

"Twenty fathoms!"

The mate at the anchor windlass repeated the order and the chain inched through the hawse pipe.

"Let go starboard anchor!"

The *Mayfair* now stood fast to two lines, her stern just out from the end of the chute. Her skipper was getting signals from shore and he was prepared to slacken the starboard anchor chain to allow the stern to move directly under the chute and swing on a forty-degree arc.

The tide was full high now. When it ebbed he would have to change the ship's position. With a south wind, the reef rocks protected her, but if the wind increased to near gale force the skipper was aware that the seas would hurdle the rocks and crash down upon the little schooner. But his calculations had the wind shifting to westward and decreasing in violence.

Now a man was catfooting down the chute with careless attention to the ropes which ran shoulder-high along the swinging, jerking structure. At the lower tip he stood on a little platform and raised a hand, shouting:

"Hallo, you—*Mayfair!* Who are you, Captain?"

"Captain Olsen," he shouted in return. "Steam schooner *Mayfair* out of Benecia. I can take eighty thousand feet below decks, ten on top. How much you got?"

"Over a hundred thousand. Boss says to pack it on."

"I'll take what I can. What destination?"

"Honolulu."

"Start loading. We'll chance the blow."

He watched the man on the shaky chute with full admiration. He had climbed the rigging of many unsteady sailing ships, walked the footropes on the yards when the masts were doing crazy dances and certain death waited below. Now he thought he would be glad to do that again rather than handle the job this man had to do.

The clapperman signaled the crew at the head of the chute and pieces of lumber began sliding down, stopping against a shoe which the man held tight with a lever. Then when the *Mayfair*'s stern swung under his swaying perch, he yanked the lever to let the timber drop to the deck. As the schooner swung back, three boards clattered down before open water showed again.

Lumber continued to slide down the chute, which lurched and tugged at the guy lines under the powerful gusts of wind. The clapperman had his feet braced solidly, hands clasped tightly around the lever. The *Mayfair* changed her position slightly with the ebbing tide but the piles of lumber on her deck kept growing faster than the crew could stow it below.

At the change of watch Captain Olsen went to his cabin for a rest without taking off his clothes. He was uneasy. The weather, instead of settling to the fair side, was getting thicker and wilder. He went to sleep to the groans of his ship and the booming sounds of lumber dropping. Only minutes later, it seemed, the mate was shaking him awake. The *Mayfair* was pitching and bucking. Torrents of rain were battering at the cabin.

"Better take over, Captain. She can't hold fast much longer."

Outside in the tortured night Captain Midnight saw the rain bucketing down with mad, hurricane force. The gale had turned into a westerly rain squall, sea water leaping to meet the sheets falling out of black skies. Shoreward, the flimsy lumber chute, barely discernible in the rain and smother of black smoke from the schooner's stack, was jumping and jerking like a frightened horse. Below it the breakers crashed and exploded on the rocks. From all sides the sounds were deafening.

Trapped in the dog hole, the *Mayfair* clung desperately to her two anchor lines. To a man captain and crew knew what would happen if either anchor let go or even slipped a few fathoms. The ship would be matchwood in an hour, the men pounded to death in the smashing, bashing breakers. Captain Midnight met the challenge.

"Start the engines," he ordered the crew below.

It was a safety precaution. He had no intention of moving out of this anchorage, precarious as it was, even assuming the schooner could get out. But if the anchors did give way, she would be ready to keep up the pressure against the storm. Midnight Olsen knew he would have less than a minute to get the ship under way before she was caught in the breakers. Now ordering all hands on deck, he set a double watch on the anchor lines with orders to report any slippage at once, lit his pipe, and waited. What happened next was not in his calculations.

"Barge to starboard!"

It was the mate's voice, slamming on his ears over the howl of the squall and the swish of rain and sea. Captain Midnight leaped to the rail and saw, cavorting in the wild chop, a thirty-foot barge. It could have come from nowhere but the river and he instantly knew it had broken loose from its sawmill moorage on the flood tide. Anyone less than a shipmaster could now tell what was bound to happen with the barge running wild in the dog hole.

"Half speed ahead."

The order was against his better judgment and against all good rules of navigation. By putting the ship ahead he was disturbing her ground tackle. The anchors were holding and would hold better with the pull of the schooner on them. But the loose barge had created an emergency.

As he watched the big bulk it was suddenly lifted high on a crest and came crashing down on the *Mayfair*'s forepeak. Then it fell back for another blow and the bow anchor chain hung limp.

"Haul in starboard anchor!"

The *Mayfair* had seaway now and was struggling valiantly against all the noisy, savage forces set to annihilate her. But there was no control for the barge. It was a great club in the hands of a demon—ten tons of wild fury. It smashed against the schooner's beam, fell off and battered her bow again. Then as she made slow headway across the turbulent dog hole, it struck a glancing blow on the stern, turned turtle, flopped down on the gear and after rail, then with a grinding lunge carried away half the deckhouse, and slithered off into the sea.

The sturdy little *Mayfair* was at last free from the battering ram but Captain Midnight Olsen was using all his skill and ingenuity to keep his ship off the rocks on either side. Then above the wail and clamor of the squall he heard another splintering crash. Through the spray and flying scud he saw the barge flung against the cliffs. As it split, one great section flew high, tearing the lower half of the lumber chute away from its guy lines and spilling it into the breakers. He knew that was the end of any further lumber loading.

The *Mayfair* picked her wallowing way clear of the rocks and headed out to sea. Here she had only the wind and waves to fight, no thrashing wild thing, and no rocks to contend with. And she rode out the storm safely. At her San Francisco wharf, unloading the few feet of redwood which would barely pay for the damage to the deck and house, word came from the Navarro River sawmill that the lumber chute was being rebuilt and in a month the *Mayfair* could return for another cargo. Captain Midnight Olsen chewed on his pipe and said dryly to the mill's agent:

"I'll get the cargo but put it in the agreement to burn all the barges they got. I can't bargain to whip something that don't fight in a seamanlike fashion."

VI

California . . . 1872

"ELLSWORTH'S FOLLY"

GOLD was good to Clem Ellsworth—at first. He was rich at the age of twenty-two. And then like so many pioneers and miners in California's early days, he kept on mining and suddenly had lost his small fortune.

As a boy in Maine, Clem had heard about the great Gold Rush of 1849 and when an uncle in the California mines sent for him, he eagerly took passage on a four-masted bark and eighty-two days later landed in San Francisco. The boy went north by stage to the Mount Shasta country and at the Eagle Creek diggings he and his uncle struck gold. Clem Ellsworth's share was over twenty thousand dollars. Then he sank his money in another mining venture near Copper City and found himself head over heels in debt.

Now Clem's real destiny took hold. He was strong and had learned to work hard, so he went from one mining camp to another, whipsawing lumber for mine timbers and sluice boxes. This was all wearisome hand work but he kept doggedly at it until he had paid off his debts.

He began to see his future in lumbering, not gold mining, which was natural for a boy from the Maine woods. All around him in this new California was great opportunity in cutting and selling lumber from the millions of acres of the various species of pine.

In 1866 he built a sawmill on the south fork of Clear Creek in Shasta County, one which used the steam for power. The water flowed over a big paddle wheel and turned the crude machinery. But although he owned his own business at twenty-nine, he had really just begun a career, for he had dreams of building a "lumber empire."

"C. F.," a man said to him one day, "why do you fool around with this measly scrub timber? Why don't you go into that virgin pine down by Chico? There's big money to be made there."

The young lumberman took a trip through the timber mentioned and agreed with his friend. At Wakefield's Station on the Chico and Humboldt wagon road, he set up a portable sawmill, one that could be kept close to the trees as they were cut out. This venture was so successful in the few years following that C. F. was able to build, at Butte Meadows, his now famous "empire." And he named it Empire Mill.

Young Ellsworth continued to have visions, however, not only of more wealth but of a way to get lumber to the new railroad at Chico without having to use slow, uncertain wagon trains. The picture forming in his mind was of a lumber flume—an overhead trough of water on which boards could float and travel piece by piece for dozens of miles.

"It's a grand scheme, Mr. Ellsworth," the local surveyor told him, "but you can't build it here. Such a flume would have to be raised on trestles of varying heights. The

Union Lumber Company Collection

ABOVE: It took raw courage to enter and anchor in the dog holes of the wild Mendocino Coast. *(Pages 57-58)*. BELOW: "Ellsworth's Folly"—a successful lumber flume."

A. A. Lausmann

ABOVE: Saws had to be welded end-to-end to cut the redwoods. *(Page 77)*. BELOW: "It was a constant battle . . . until the bulls became tangled and the driver stopped the team." *(Page 80)*.

Romans used stone, but you would have to use pine timber. And how are you going to put wooden trestles on the sides of those lava-flow gorges around here?"

But such handicaps as these only made the dream of a flume more desirable to sawmiller Ellsworth. The whole idea began to control his thinking. If he couldn't build such a water line here, he would sell his holdings and move where a flume *could* be built. And so he sold and bought another sawmill—the old Champion mill in Tehama County—and here he was to see the fulfillment of his dream. A forty-mile-long elevated water conduit was built to carry lumber from mill to market. Yet this great structure of beauty and utility was, in the eyes of other sawmill men, a costly and foolhardy method that would never work.

"This man Ellsworth," they said, "hasn't got good sense. Any normal person would know that contraption won't work. Look at all the money it cost, and it's going to cost more to keep water running through it. By the time his lumber gets to the railroad, it will be worth its weight in gold dust."

So the flume became known as "Ellsworth's Folly."

But whatever its name and value, the flume was a great engineering achievement of that day—the year 1872. It took three years to build at an estimated cost of five thousand dollars a mile, or $200,000 for the full length. The line started at ground level in a mountain meadow below the sawmill and crossed high over gullies and chasms, ending in a long, flat traverse of a valley floor at Sesma, which was the nearest point it could meet the railroad on the east side of the Sacramento River.

The flume was actually a V-shaped trough, with the bottom of the V flattened. It was sixteen inches wide at this bottom, with the sides flaring out to forty-eight inches apart at the top or water line. The trough rested on A-shaped trestles even where it curled around the sheer sides of rocky gulches. Its elevation from the ground varied to allow an average drop of twenty-seven feet to the mile. This grade however was only maintained on the engineer's blueprints. At one point—Grecian Bend—the drop was so sharp the water flowed forty miles an hour and at other points it was difficult to force it to flow at all.

C. F. Ellsworth's sawmill was its own best customer during the building of the flume, as it consumed enough lumber to build a small city of houses. There were many miles of curves where the reinforcement of "drag boards" or plank linings was necessary on bottoms and sides to keep the speeding lumber from breaking through.

Owner Ellsworth was justly proud of his great snakelike trough crawling along bottoms and meadows, then crossing a gulch to seemingly cling to the mountainside more than a hundred feet above the river bed. Visitors and lumber buyers would marvel at the sight as C. F. stood below the mill's lumber deck and started a bundle of boards, timbers, or shakes on the forty-mile journey.

"Now folks," he would say with his hand held high, "some of our lumber is floated down by the piece. 'Specially the low-grade boards." Then he would slide a few ten-foot planks off the pile and toss them in the coursing water. He would watch them disappear in the distance and then turn to his crew.

"Boys—you ready with that bundle? This, folks, is how

the better quality of lumber is sent down. You see, it's a sort of raft, the boards clamped together. The part that's in the water is common lumber, the top boards are choice grades." And the raft would be launched with a great splash, the bulky bundle bobbing and slewing down the trough.

The proud owner did not tell everybody—only his closest friends—that many thousands of pieces and bundles never arrived at Sesma. Unable to get around some of the bad curves, they tumbled over the sides of the flume, to split and splinter on the rocks far down in the bottom of a chasm.

Such accidents broke out whole sections of the flume. All the water then flowed out and continued to flow out until the break was repaired. During all this time no lumber could be sent down. Ellsworth built cabins every few miles for the flume tenders or "lumber herders," whose job it was to patrol the structure, walking along narrow footboards beside the trough. The tenders kept the line in the best repair they could and cleared jams of lumber when they occurred.

When lumber was being flumed at night, a herder hung an empty coal-oil can on a rope across the top of the trough. As long as the can kept rattling, the herder knew the lumber was coming down all right. If there was no sound and he found lumber was not flowing down, he began patrolling upflume to find out what was wrong. Since the flume was often a hundred feet in the air, and the footboards were apt to be slick with frost and spray, he was in constant danger of falling to his death.

Lumber, shakes, and cordwood were not the only

cargoes floated down. There were no telegraph lines in those early days and requests for supplies at the sawmill were tacked on the lumber bundles and the supplies were later brought up by wagon. When a sawmill worker or one of his family was injured or became desperately ill, the victim was placed in a "flume boat" and speeded down to some doctor in the valley. Household goods were also moved out of the high country in these crafts, which more than once met with disaster when rounding a sharp turn or striking a projecting sliver of wood.

Such a boat ride offered never-to-be-forgotten thrills. The boats were V-shaped to fit the flume and as the occupants sat in them they were above the sides of the flume. Always facing them was the danger of the boat snagging on a loose board or going through a break in the flume. Sometimes the craft would run ahead of the flow of water and then, when the water came cascading up to it, the boat would be sent forward with a great jerk that could easily catapult the riders over the flume sides. Should the boat be stranded, with the flow of water cut off, the riders had to climb out and walk like careful cats along the footboard until they reached the next tender's station, where they could descend by a crude ladder to the ground.

One flume rider wrote:

> It was a ride beyond my wildest imagination. There were probably fifty men from the mill standing around waiting to see us off. Four big fellows held the eight-foot boat over the flume and told us to jump into it the minute it touched the water and to "hang on to your hats!"

The signal of all-ready was given, the boat was dropped and we leaped into it the best we could, which was not very smoothly, Arthur landing on one knee and shoulder and I on his legs. One man who helped launch the boat slipped and fell on the stern of it. He managed to roll out on the trestle and we were too busy unscrambling ourselves to see whether or not he was hurt.

The terrors of that ride will never be blotted from the memories of either of us. To ride upon the cow-catcher of a locomotive down a steep grade or even upon a level one is simply exhilarating. You know there is a wide track laid upon a firm foundation, that there are wheels grooved and fitted to the track, that there are trusty men at the brakes, and better than all, you know that the power that impels the train can be instantly shut off by a hand on the lever.

But a flume has no element of safety. There is no evenness of grade, no regulation of speed for you to go fast or slow at your pleasure. You are wholly at the mercy of the water. You cannot stop, you cannot lessen your speed, you have nothing to hold on to; you have only to sit still, shut your eyes, say your prayers, take all the water and spray that comes—drenching you, filling the boat—and wait for eternity. I cannot give a better idea of a flume boat ride than to compare it to sliding down an eave trough hanging in mid-air without support and to keep on it for forty miles.

At the start we went at the rate of about fifteen miles an hour, then we slowed down. Arthur sat in front on the bottom and I behind on the seat in the stern, which was a great service to Arthur in keeping from him the water which broke over the end. Unlike any other boat we were pushed by the water, rather than riding on top of it. Of course, when we went shooting down the steeper grades, Arthur took great splashes of water. The effect then was like riding on a bumpy rain cloud.

In this ride, which fails me to describe, I was perched up in a boat no wider than a chair, sometimes twenty feet in the air, sometimes seventy and more. When the spray would enable me to look ahead, I would see this ribbon of a trough here and there for miles, so small and narrow, and apparently so fragile, that I could compare it only to a chalk mark high in the air on which I was traveling at frantic speed.

One circumstance during the trip did more to unnerve me than anything else. We had been rushing down at a pretty lively rate of speed, when the bow of the boat very suddenly struck something—a nail or lodged stick of wood. What was the result? Arthur was upended on his face and I on his back.

But we continued to rush along; minutes seemed hours. Actually it seemed a full hour before we reached the worst place in the flume but Arthur tells me it was less than ten minutes. The flume at this point took a terrifying pitch and if the truth must be known, I was scared almost out of reason. However I yet had a morbid curiosity to see how fast we were going and I huddled down as low as I could, keeping my eyes on the hills. Every object was gone before I could clearly see what it was. I felt that I weighed no more than a feather.

Now we were suddenly slowed down and fairly crept along until I thought we would surely ground to a stop. The only water in the trough was in the very bottom. We were presently saved from this condition by a replenishment of our water supply, which came in surges and jerked us along like riding on a hobbled burro. Then the grade would steepen and again we would be scooting along smoothly if not securely. Now would come long stretches where the trestles rode close to the ground and we took the opportunity to breathe deeply.

This only remains to be said. We made the entire length of the flume in about three and a half hours and I doubt if there is a power on earth which would impel me to take the ride again. Needless to say I am not a sawmill worker for Mr. Ellsworth or required to ride the flume for any other reason.

We had been told we could see flume tenders along the way but we did not. We saw one of their cabins and three little children staring at us like scared barn cats from the brush of a dry creek bed. Since a flag had been sent down a bundle of lumber saying that was the last one to be sent and that a boat was coming instead, the flume tenders probably deserted their jobs for a while thinking human beings did not need tending like valuable lumber did.

Arthur and I were a wet and weak pair when we pulled ourselves out of the boat at Sesma. Arthur said he was quite willing to leave the flume to the timber and took to his bed, unable to eat supper. I saw to getting our clothes made respectable and followed him.

This was "Ellsworth's Folly," which in fact was very successful—a folly only to those who scorned the daring idea. By 1873, forty thousand feet of lumber were flowing down the flume every day and a planing mill was erected at Sesma to handle it. The flume pioneered in covering the wide gap between mill and railroad and was the forerunner of other water lines.

However C. F. Ellsworth's creation was in a sense a folly to him. In 1873 he fell from the flume, suffering severe shock and fatal injuries. Shortly after this his company passed into other hands.

VII

California . . . 1881

BOY LOGGER OF MILL CREEK

IF C. R. Johnson had not found a friend to go prospecting the redwoods with him, the first seventy years of Pacific Coast lumbering history would have taken a far different turn. As it was the redheaded boy and the family friend did take a stagecoach ride that was to result in the Union Lumber Company's empire.

In San Francisco lay C. Russell Johnson's destiny. He was a lively fourteen-year-old in Saugatuck, Michigan, and Racine, Wisconsin, when he suddenly fell ill and was forced to leave school. Sent to San Francisco to recover, he spent hours in his uncle's auction store and in others too, learning the amazing facts about the new West, regaining his health in two years. He was strong enough now to work for his father, who by this time, 1877, was logging and running a sawmill in the French-Canadian area of St. Ignace, Michigan. Then he spent four years with a Chicago lumber firm.

But the free spirit of the West had found its way into C. R.'s blood. San Francisco, growing fast after the gold rush, its harbor filled with sailing ships carrying exotic cargoes, had made a strong impression on him. Since he had come of age, he returned to the city by the Golden Gate—a lumberman looking for new woods to conquer. He went to see A. D. Starr, a friend of his father's, who operated a flour mill in the little town of Crockett.

"Mr. Starr," he said, "you've often told me about these redwood trees out here, how big they are and everything. They won't believe those stories back home. I want to believe you, but how can I when you say twenty men holding hands can't reach around some of them?"

"Maybe twenty-one men, son." The flour miller laughed. "Well, whether you or those scoffers back home believe it or not, the size of those trees is tremendous. There was one up on the Russian River I saw cut down. It was twenty-three feet in diameter and three hundred feet long lying there on the ground. A fellow named English chopped it down after two weeks' work and he got six hundred thousand shingles out of it. Son—that tree was over three thousand years old. Think of it!"

All this was beyond C. R.'s understanding when the largest tree he had ever seen in Michigan's pine woods was three feet in diameter. He shook his head in bewilderment. His older friend took him by the shoulder.

"Go ahead, C. R., and call me a liar. I wouldn't blame you. But if you do, I'll sure make you eat your words when you learn I'm right. It looks now like I've got to back up my tales. Tell you what. Next week we'll start out and look. Maybe take two weeks. I'd like to see more of those beautiful woods myself."

"Are there very many men cutting the trees yet?"

"Thirty years ago the Russians at Fort Ross cut a lot of them, used them for buildings, and sold a lot of lumber and shingles. Then the gold strike got people's minds off trees but on the other hand brought a lot of men to California that see the possibilities of redwood. Now there's some kind of a sawmill on every river running into the ocean. I'd say maybe twenty—big and small. Like Gualala, Elk Creek, Navarro, Salmon Creek, Albion, Little River, Big River, Russian Gulch, and so on. But you'll see."

The two set off by buckboard stage from Cloverdale to Navarro, threading their way up the timbered valleys and over bare hills, arriving at the river mouth settlement in a driving rainstorm. Moving in and out of the magnificent, towering stands of the red-barked trees had opened C. R. Johnson's eyes with wonder. What he couldn't believe before he now saw and A. D. Starr had not exaggerated. Nothing but the word *massive* could describe them better and now nothing like a little rain was going to dampen his enthusiasm. He had never hoped to see such beautiful, stately pillars of growing wood. They were poetic in their grandeur, these bushy-topped redwoods—the oldest living things on the earth.

"We've got to keep going, Mr. Starr," he told his companion. "I can't get enough of this. I've talked to a man here who has a wagon and team he'll hire out to us."

The flour miller gave in and drenched as they were, they hired the rig and made slow, rough progress northward along the coast, fording rivers or ferrying where they could on crude *bateaux*. They were bound for the abandoned Army post of Fort Bragg and beyond it the thriving little lumber colony of Westport.

They did not reach it. At Ten Mile River they overtook a wagonload of lumber. The teamster said it was from

Stewart and Hunter's sawmill and he was hauling it to the shipping point of Newport on the sea at the mouth of Ten Mile. C. R. and his guide turned upriver and then up Mill Creek, staying overnight at the sawmill.

It was a lucky turn. Brothers-in-law Calvin Stewart and James Hunter were affable young men and glad to have such personable visitors. C. R. made friends with them immediately. He watched the little sawmill operate, tramped for a day through the timber, rode a wagonload of lumber down to Newport where a sailing schooner was being loaded by means of a wooden chute extending from the high bluff down over the ship's deck. Then he asked:

"Would you men like a partner?"

Calvin Stewart blinked and James Hunter hurled a redwood cone in the creek. Both were inwardly elated, but as businessmen were not too eager to show it.

"We might," Hunter said.

"How much would it cost—say, a one-third interest?"

This brought on a full discussion and when all were agreed the third partner was a good idea, a price was set for that share. C. R. shook hands with the two and climbed up on the seat of the rig with A. D. Starr.

"I'll get the money," he said, "and I'll be back here as soon as I have it. I'll leave right away for my home in Michigan."

He did and he was back in six weeks. His father could not be convinced of the great timber chance C. R. had in mind, considering it too good to be true. There just couldn't be trees yielding three hundred thousand feet of lumber! Ridiculous! But he had faith in his red-haired son and arranged the money transfer. The name of the new firm was Stewart, Hunter and Johnson and C. R. was a partner at twenty-three.

Now the hard work began. It was a day and a country where there was no other kind if a man wanted to keep on eating and retain any self-respect—an age when men never expected something for nothing. The men in these redwoods were used to hard work and not afraid to use every muscle as long as it was necessary. Brains had their place but hands were always there to back them up.

C. R. went out with the tree-felling crew. It was early spring and from now until the fall rains began most of the trees would be laid down. The crew consisted of choppers, sawyers, bark peelers, and cook. The head chopper selected a tree for its lumber quality and ease of felling, marking out a path so it would come down with the least damage to itself and others. C. R. quickly learned that many thousand feet of fine trees could be ruined if the fall was not clean and on a flat surface, that the wood was very brittle and easily rifted. The trunk must lie where others would not fall on it.

A staging was built eight or ten feet from the ground, above the spread of roots. The sawyers mounted the platform and made the undercut with saws longer than the young lumberman thought it possible to make them—this one almost twenty feet long. The sawing was done on the side of the tree toward which it was to fall, cutting into a third of the diameter. Then armed with hickory-handled, double-bitted axes weighing four pounds, the choppers began carving out giant chips high enough above the undercut to form a triangle with it as the axes bit into the great bole of the tree.

It took four days to chop out the undercut of this first tree, sixteen feet in diameter, and then the sawyers made the falling cut on the opposite side of the trunk, slightly above the undercut line. As the saw wore in, with the dry, almost sapless dust spilling out on the knee-deep pile of chips, the men with mauls drove iron wedges in behind it to force the tree to lean and keep from binding the saw. When it approached the halfway point, the two-thousand-year-old monarch, groaning as its life was nearly ended, its fibers snapping and cracking, leaned farther out as the wedges were hammered in deeper. Then the gigantic bulk strained, trembled, and came crashing down with a deafening, earth-shaking explosion. It was a sight and sound young Johnson never could have believed possible. For five minutes he stood stunned beyond action. Then suddenly he was aware that the head chopper was barking at him:

"You come to work or stare? Take one of them bars and follow that fellow there. He'll show you how to peel bark."

At twelve- to twenty-foot spaces the bole of the felled tree was being marked for bucking—rings made around the girth as guides for sawing. Ax men opened the bark and peelers attacked it with heavy, strap-iron bars which had been pounded to a thin edge. C. R. thought he had worked hard but this was the most grueling, back-breaking labor he ever wanted to do. That night he fell into his bunk without supper and slept in exhaustion.

At five in the morning he ate enough for two men and went bark-peeling again, while the sawyers sectioned the tree and made the logs ready for the bull teams. They moved with the choppers to a new tree and were replaced by men with jackscrews, mauls, and snatch blocks, who rolled the peeled logs out where the bulls could get at them. A crew of swampers had already brushed out a road to Mill Creek and the chain-tenders came along with the oxen—six of them—huge and showing unlimited power at every plodding step.

"You can pack water," the bull driver told the young logger as he strode in between the animals, helping to yoke them into pairs with heavy, hand-hewn blocks fitted with two iron loops which went around the bulls' necks. "There's tanks along the road. You fill the cans and splash water under the head log. Keep it sliding in mud. Watch out for them bulls' feet."

The log sections had been sniped, sharp corners of the forward end beveled off so as not to "hang up" on roots or hummocks in the road. Iron spikes or "dogs" with chains attached were driven into each end of the logs, coupling them together.

"Hi-yup! Ben! Smart!"

The bull driver slapped his goad stick against the flanks of two bulls, prodding them into the lead with the end of the goad which was studded with a small, sharp nail, then lining the other four animals behind them. A long chain was threaded between the bulls and attached to the lead log.

"Hup—you lazy brutes! Press—in there. Now—Smart— Ben. Arr-rr-up!"

A sharp jab into the near leader's ribs jerked him into action, then the off leader jumped with him. The others followed in slow procession. The chain came taut and the bull driver was goading, shouting, cursing, and running back and forth in a noisy show of power. The team lurched ahead and the first log stirred. The bulls felt the pull, dug in, the second and succeeding logs moving slowly forward. The train was underway down the slight grade, chains clanking above the driver's shouts, the whole cavalcade enveloped in a smothering cloud of dust.

C. R. ran ahead to the water tank and filled his big tin bucket. There was no need to tell him to be careful of the bulls' hoofs. They came slashing back with a force that would cut like a knife and crush any bones in their way. He darted in behind them and dumped his bucket under the first log, dashing back for more water. It was a constant battle to make mud of the deep dust until the bulls became tangled and the driver stopped the team to get them in order again. By the time the train was halfway to the river bank, the logs were sliding well, the driver's yells were less frequent, and C. R.'s shirt and trousers were a mass of mud. He knew there was easier work but none so exhilarating. He was a pioneer in redwood lumbering and here he would stay.

The landing crew unhooked the bulls from their chains and they were herded back along the road. Jackscrews were wedged in under the sides of the logs and the big bulks rolled over the banks, plummeting into the river where boomsticks formed a sort of corral.

For a month C. R. Johnson worked as a sugler, or water packer, and in that short time saw many operations which could be simplified, shortened, or eliminated. Later he took his cut with the broadax and helped build scaffolds at the bases of the redwood giants. He worked with the chain tenders and landing crews and out on the floating logs.

In the fall, when the rains set in and the rivers started to rise, the logs choked them from bank to bank. One day they were set free to bump and buck downstream into the boom at the sawmill. The circular saw blades reduced them to timbers and boards which horse teams hauled to the shipping point on the headlands. The youngest partner of Stewart, Hunter and Johnson knew this was the weak spot of the enterprise.

"Calvin—Jim," he said one night after about six months of apprenticeship, "this is no place for a mill, and loading steamers piece by piece with the flimsy kind of chute we have is the slowest, costliest method I could imagine. Listen now. When I was roaming around last month I saw just the place we ought to have our mill—level land, a good harbor, and back of it timber on Pudding Creek and the Noyo River fit for a king's dream. It's by that old Army post—Fort Bragg. The cove is called Soldier's Harbor."

The partners knew it well and C. R. went on with his romancing. "I'll take soundings in the harbor and see if big ships can get in there. If so we'll build a wharf—and maybe a wire chute to handle bundles of boards, five or six thousand feet at a time. And I can see ahead a few years to the time when we'll have a donkey engine logging for us, like this new one Mr. Dolbeer has invented, and we'll even build a railroad back into the timber as we cut it out. If we can reach Willits with it, we can ship lumber right to San Francisco by rail."

To the older partners it was all a fantastic vision but

the more they thought about it, the more they realized their redheaded associate's dreams were far from idle ones. His ideas were sound. They agreed in general to his plan, but asked:

"Where is the money coming from, to buy the timber, survey the harbor, build the wharf and wire chute, buy the donkey engine, and hire bigger crews?" C. R. Johnson had an answer.

"I'll get it in Michigan."

And he got it in Michigan—by selling stock to two large investors—and the Fort Bragg Redwood Company went forward. All of C. R.'s ideas proved workable, the new sawmill at Fort Bragg cutting more lumber in a twelve-hour shift than the little one on Mill Creek had in a week. This mill burned and was immediately rebuilt. The wharf, wire chute, and railroad developed. And through the years the company progressed into the Union Lumber Company with a subsidiary, the National Steamship Company, which chartered and purchased steam schooners. It weathered business depressions, fire, earthquakes, and became the huge, successful enterprise envisioned by a boy with red hair who had almost died of a heart ailment at fourteen.

VIII

Washington . . . 1884

BOILED BEEF AND BEANS AT DAYLIGHT

CYRUS WALKER never liked to be second to anybody in any activity, unless in being second he was on his way to being first. He had been boss of the Pope and Talbot woods crews and sawmills on Puget Sound for twenty-three years. He was richer than he had ever dreamed of being as part owner of the company, and he had private timber holdings. His loggers, sawmill workers, the mills themselves, the fleet of P and T ships, his big mansion on the hill at Port Ludlow—everything in the Walker domain was the best.

And so, this July twenty-second in 1884 was a big day for the tall, lean, full-bearded man who ruled the Pope and Talbot empire. On this day he was to launch the most powerful tow boat ever built in the United States—the tug *Tyee,* 140 feet of beauty and utility.

Yankee-bred Cyrus Walker had fierce pride in this newest ship in the company's fleet. He himself had selected the logs from which his Port Ludlow sawmill had cut the beams, planks, and all other wood used. He set his keen eye on the tug as she sat in her shipyard cradle—the Pope and Talbot shipyard at Port Ludlow—all ready to slide down the ways.

"Mr. Ahlquist," he said to one of the important lumber buyers who had arrived the day before on the barkentine *Klickitat,* "you see before you a noble creation—staunch and strong to stand the buffeting of the seas. Why, do you know, sir—her hull is two feet thick."

A short man had stepped quickly along the dock and now tugged at the manager's black coat sleeve. He was the shipyard foreman.

"Cy," he said cautiously, "tomorrow's the big day. Lot going on. Everybody excited. Things might get out of hand. Besides that, I just heard a boatload of ragamuffins is due here from Seattle—low-grade men and women with a lot of likker. Might be trouble."

The gray eyes became merry. "Don't worry, Mr. Peters. What trouble can they cause that we can't handle? Tomorrow all three mills—Port Gamble, Utsalady, and this one—will be shut tight. I want everybody to have a good time."

"Sure—a good time." Foreman Peters frowned. "But—there's another thing too. The boxing match—the fight we always have when a ship is in, between the sailors and the sawmill fellows. With everything else going on, are you going to allow that too?"

"Certainly, certainly, Mr. Peters. It's a holiday and I say I want everybody to have a good time. We're not going to let anybody beat us there. I'm going to have a good time—and I'll be watching things too. It will be a big day."

And the big day started early. Long before daylight the Chinese cookhouse crews were roasting sides of beef and baking hams, pies, and cakes by the hundreds, preparing the great caldrons of coffee, and rolling out barrels of beer. At sunrise with the booming of the cannon on the spacious lawn of Cyrus Walker's Admiralty Hall all kinds of boats began arriving. They carried the men out of the woods and mills, even friendly Indians—all eager for fun. A holiday for men who worked hard was a gala occasion and they intended to play just as hard as they worked.

For work hard they did. At Port Ludlow a man could be sure of $30 a month for a twelve-hour day. He could have a roof over his head and hot meals. But he would have to work for them. The mill whistle split the foggy gray chill at twenty minutes past five. Twenty minutes later it blew again and the men sat down to a breakfast of boiled beef, potatoes, baked beans, hash, griddle cakes, biscuits, and coffee. At the six-o'clock whistle, saws were turning, logs and boards booming along the rolls in the wet, sawdust-filled air. And twelve hours later—every day—the men were paid spot cash at the company store.

But now the *Tyee* was to be launched and no one was thinking of work. By noon the milling throngs included officers from the *Klickitat* in gaudy uniform, deck hands from the sailing ship and tugs in port, shipbuilding crews and company bosses. Then there were the visiting dignitaries and frock-coated lumber buyers parading with their bustled ladies.

Two thousand people sat down to the feast and stuffed themselves to the bursting point. Afterward some of them moved to the baseball field, some to the dock where old ships' sails had been stretched tight over the planking and battened down. A band struck up "Oh, Susanna" and couples pranced in lively step.

Whistles sounded at the shipyard and the celebrants streamed around the end of the sawmill to the ways on the sandy point. High above them, stern toward the water, rested the 140-foot *Tyee,* her bare hull draped with bunting and ready for her short slide into the bay. Flags waved from a dozen vessels. The band played "Over the Waves." Shouts and shrieks rose from the excited crowd.

Cyrus Walker walked forward with dignified stride and handed a bottle of wine to the little girl beside him. As he raised his hand the music hung on an extended note and the girl crashed the bottle against the *Tyee*'s prow. A great cheer went up as the chocks were knocked from beneath her hull.

The tug slid down smoothly and struck the water with a great splash. The wave set all other craft in violent motion, washing up over the spit and breaking into the squealing crowd. There was another cheer as the *Tyee* swung broadside to a blast of whistles and boom of drums.

Then the host of watchers seemed strangely silent except for a few scattered shouts. The show was over and the crowd was turning toward the mill or walking slowly back toward the dance floor. Then some stopped and looked out into the bay once more. Another drama was taking place.

A small tug was standing by to tow the helpless *Tyee* back to the shipyard. But now, from around the point, a little workboat was chugging out, her decks swarming with wildly yelling men and women. A man in the bow was whirling a manila line around his head. Almost before the crowd was aware of it another had leaped on the *Tyee*'s empty deck and was securing the line. He leaped back as the workboat engine roared. The *Tyee* was under tow—headed for the open Sound!

"Look—they're stealing it!"

"What boat is that?"

Cyrus Walker and those with him were astonished beyond belief. Yet there was no question about it—the nameless workboat had the precious *Tyee* underway, however slowly, and the people on her were hooting and caterwauling to a faretheewell.

The jeers sent the lean, black-coated figure into action. He sped down the dock, hailing the company tug *Yakima* which had already started in pursuit of the hapless *Tyee*. Seeing Cyrus Walker waving his arms, the skipper reversed his engines and put back to take him aboard. The lumber king was irate.

"That's those rapscallions from Seattle!" he bellowed. "Drunk and disorderly. What are they trying to do? Everybody will think I ordered this. All right, Captain—let's get them!"

There was no malice, only an excited twinkle in Cyrus Walker's eye as the chase began. Ahead, the small towing craft was breasting the waves in open water but was held steady by the drag of the big *Tyee* which it was just able to keep in the seaway. Swiftly the powerful *Yakima,* built to tow great sailing ships and log booms, went in pursuit. She was abreast of the *Tyee* in a twinkling as the workboat's passengers yelled her on. As she closed in on them, a volley of bottles, gear, and boat hooks came flying.

"Give her more steam, *Yakima!*" they shouted. "That's Cy Walker in her. Hey, you—Cy, we're putting your new *Tyee* in commission!"

As the words came hurtling back at the company manager, the *Yakima* pressing hard on the beam of the bobbing workboat, the line to the *Tyee* flew apart. With the drag released, the overburdened craft wallowed in a bow wave.

"You can have her now, Cyrus!" someone in the motley crew shouted. "Hooray for Mr. Walker and his *Tyee!*"

Their boat pitched again and some of the riffraff were jostled to the rail. As the pilot tried to get the craft under control a cross wave struck it and two women went head-long over the side, clutching at a man and pulling him in with them.

Two hands on the *Yakima* had boathooks out at once and the three floundering figures were pulled in almost before the ducking had soaked fright into them. The *Tyee* was secured to a tow line once more as the workboat turned to and ran with the sea. Cyrus Walker wore a grin as he surveyed the half-drowned would-be pirates.

"Well, you had your fun and there's no harm done. Let's get back to moorage, Captain. I have work to do."

Once on the wharf he turned his attention to his invited guests. He had the place to entertain them—the finest baronial home in the entire Puget Sound country. High atop the hill, on acres of green lawn, where the cannon thundered salutes to Pope and Talbot ships as they arrived in the bay, was Admiralty Hall. This was Cyrus Walker's castle, complete with white picket fence, cupola, and doors that slid open as in a ship's cabin. This estate was where he wined and dined agents of foreign lumber buyers, ship captains, world travelers, and railroad kings. The great rooms, galleries, and food cellars were in the full Walker tradition, filled with the finest furnishings and supplies.

The owner of all this glowed with a sense of well-being as he relaxed in the library, his visitors sipping their brandy and smoking their Havana cigars. The day had been an important one in his life. His pride and joy, the *Tyee,* was ready to be fitted out and soon would be paying for her cost. And as he sighed contentedly, the men who had logged the timber and cut the beams for her with sweat and struggle were just starting the kind of rough-and-ready celebration they wanted—a fight.

The arrival of a vessel at Port Ludlow always called for a bloody contest. The top fighter of the ship challenged the strongest and handiest of the millworkers or longshoremen. Now the *Klickitat* was moored and her sailors were spoiling for a chance to show their animal superiority over the landlubbing "haybacks." The timbermen were not ready to admit any such prowess.

"A crippled sailmaker could lick the best timber wolf you got around here!"

The boast came snarling from the lips of Tam Reagan, a huge Irish seaman, who stood belligerently on the edge of the noisy crowd in the big front parlor of the boardinghouse. Cheers greeted his stormy words and he swaggered about, glowering at every man who stood fast on the sawdust floor before him. Then from deep within the crowd, a small man elbowed his way to the front. In the smelly, smoky dimness of the light from the teakettle lamps, which burned fish oil, the man was seen to be Little Archie. There were murmurings from the crowd and a few shouts:

"Go get him, Archie! Climb the big Siwash's frame!"

Even Archie Pettigrew's name was an aggravation to men who found the little fellow in their way. Yet if they took the trouble to push him aside they found they had struck a nest of hornets or worse. Archie Pettigrew, to those who knew him, was a hundred and fifty pounds of cougar crossed with dynamite and ready to battle to the teeth any man who slandered a logger. In the woods he was a sniper, a man who with an ax beveled off the forward ends of the logs so they would not hang up on the skid road as the bulls dragged them along. His arms were as hard as fir knots, his footwork as shifty as any tree cat. And now he did not like the slurred words this big Irishman was throwing around so carelessly. A quick step-and-hop landed him close to the sailor, who stood almost a head taller.

"Don't see any crippled sailmakers, so you'll do for a starter."

Archie's boots were shod with calks and faster than big Tam Reagan could step back, the calks had dug and raked at his dungareed shins. He jumped and swung a sledge-hammer fist which struck Archie a glancing blow, the force still great enough to throw the small man off balance. But before the sailor could start another swing, Archie was upon him and all over him—leaping, squirming, pounding the heavy frame with lightning-fast punches.

Reagan gasped and sputtered, hammering Archie unmercifully with his big fists but receiving in return some vicious blows and kicks where he least expected them. The roar of the crowd, the stamp of feet and pounding of bottles and glasses on the tables, lent more savagery to the battle.

Archie stepped back suddenly, bent double, and upended his man in a flurry of legs, arms, and sawdust. Blood ran from the Irishman's face and Archie Pettigrew's ear caught a pistonlike drive which all but tore it off. Reagan pinned him to the floor and would have knocked him insensible if the little logger had not squirmed free.

This time the sailor made a bulling rush and again the pair were rolling in the sawdust, Reagan panting and spitting curses, little Archie raking him with his calks. Stretched flat on his broad back, Reagan brought his leg up swiftly and the logger was caught by the violence of it. He pitched forward but both of his heavy boots, shod with steel spikes, came down on the pudgy, bristled face of his opponent. Tam Reagan yelled with pain and rage. He tried to struggle to his feet but it was too late.

The crowd could contain itself no longer. With a roar of lust it swept over both fighters. Some tried to pull Archie Pettigrew free and others tried to rescue Reagan. Then the two were forgotten in the mad, uncontrollable mob hysteria. Friends were fighting friends and enemies helping each other wrestle with whoever was twisting the neck of someone else.

A bottle came sailing through the air and set one of the teakettles into a spin. A pike pole appeared and came whacking down on a head. More bottles were thrown into the melee. The front doors could not stand against the surge of the crowd and crashed open, spilling men out on the muddy street. The pole was flayed high, knocking the smoking lamp from its chain. Flaming oil went running through the sawdust and clothes were burning on the backs of men who tried to smother the flames.

Whoops and cries broke the night air around the sawmill. From every direction came the frantic calls of "Fire!" In the panic men fell, and were trampled on.

Fighting for safety in the blackness, others tripped into the uncontrolled flames and ran in crazy circles, feeling for whatever bit of cool night air they could find. Buckets were splashed into water barrels and passed from hand to hand into the burning building—a full tub, hoisted on shoulders, was dumped into the conflagration. Axes were snatched up and swung wildly, then the heads of beer kegs were smashed in, the acrid fumes mingling with the smell of burning fish oil, sawdust, and cloth. But the fluid gushed over the floor, sloshing into the flames and over the seared, motionless bodies on the floor. They were dragged out and in a little while there was only smoke mingling with dying excitement and horror.

Cyrus Walker had heard none of this as it was happening. He had a mortal fear of fire as a power that could wipe out all he owned and controlled. When he learned of the near catastrophe in the morning and surveyed the damage, he thanked the powers above that it was no worse. Then he gave immediate orders for rebuilding the boarding-house. He looked at the men about him quizzically. "Well, boys—who won the fight?"

The only answer he got was that "probably the fire did." Some of the churchwomen were not so satisfied with his whimsical question. A council of them demanded that he prohibit any more fist fighting. He shook his head.

"I can't deprive men of play. They work hard and they are going to live hard—whatever I say or do. These men log trees and cut them up for people to build houses with. I declare, ladies—Pope and Talbot cut more lumber last month than any sawmills in the world. Now then—didn't we?"

California . . . 1885

KINGS OF CONVERSE BASIN

IMAGINE a great amphitheater of six square miles in the beautiful Sierra Nevada Mountains. Imagine the bottom of this thickly covered with trees, dominated by the giant redwoods, around the roots of which a river curled and tumbled. The redwoods stood broad and high, yet imagine how small they must have seemed to a man standing on the rim of the bowl's thousand-foot sides.

This Converse Basin in the Kings River area of California must have been an impressive sight to two San Francisco men in 1885. It was big country—big mountains, big trees, big rivers—and anything big looked good to Hiram C. Smith and A. D. Moore. They could match the big country with big ideas and big bankrolls.

Smith and Moore came out of the timber determined to log it—and they spent the next fifteen years doing so. While their reign as redwood kings was short, they were by far the flashiest, most colorful loggers the California timber ever saw. In fact the Sierra Nevada redwoods might never have been touched by saw or ax had these two San Francisco "live wires" not surveyed them with oversized binoculars.

The job of getting the big trees out of the mountain bowl would have discouraged men with good business judgment. Hiram Smith and A. D. Moore saw nothing but a challenge and a promise of glory. Difficulties? Bah! Nothing that could not be overcome. So, like feudal kings setting forth to conquer, they spent money and energy lavishly, fully in keeping with the mammoth timber they cut. They blasted the timber down to workable size and sent it by a fabulous flume to the railroad fifty-four miles away.

The Sierra Nevada redwoods were first cousins to those growing on the foggy coast of California. They grew bigger because of winter snows and hot summers, but these factors also made the wood inferior—more brittle and less compact. The Sierra area producing these mammoths was comparatively limited, no bigger than a sizable ranch.

But there was nothing small in any part of Smith and Moore or their logging. Everything was done in a "high, wide, and handsome" way. The two San Francisco plungers could not see anything as small as a dollar. It had to be a thousand dollars. They did not want ten bulls to haul the logs. They wanted a hundred.

"We need fifty cases of dynamite," a foreman told them. Moore scowled at him. "Order five hundred so we won't run short." If they were going to log big trees the company was going to do it in a big way.

Hannibal crossing the Alps was no better a showman than Hiram Smith was in getting the hundred- and two-hundred-ton redwood monarchs out of the Basin. The great bulks were so brittle that the sheer weight of their falling broke them apart and more than half the wood was not worth cutting.

"Never mind that," Smith and Moore said. "Who cares? We've got redwood enough here to last till doomsday. There's still twenty times as much wood in what's left of one of those as there is in any ordinary tree. Just cut down more of them."

That was the spirit—slaughter and waste. Cut more trees. Build bigger mills. Hire more men. This was a big operation, the owners said, and the world was going to know it. Never be niggardly about costs. Was one railroad enough to haul the logs to the hoist? If not, build another and get bigger locomotives. How about that hoist? Is it big enough and strong enough to lift those logs up and out of the Basin?

It was big enough, they decided, if the logs were blasted open. Of course, this would waste a lot of timber but even if the hoist could lift them, the sixteen- and twenty-foot logs were too big and bulky to handle in a sawmill. So the big bosses gave the order: "Blast them open with a big bang!"

They had special augers forged in Redding—ten and twelve feet long, the bits three inches in diameter. Two men mounted the log and twisted the T-handle half a turn at a time. It took them the better part of a day to bore six or seven holes down into the heart of the log. Into each hole they packed several pounds of black powder and attached long fuses to the blasting caps. The explosions, echoing back and forth between the Basin walls, made a shambles of the log. Still, enough of it could be salvaged to haul on the narrow-gauge railroad which ran to the hoist on Upper Abbott Creek.

This apparatus was ingenious and exerted tremendous power through the use of complicated gears and a counter-balance. The heavy log sections were lifted over the ridge and lowered to the transfer station from which a standard gauge railroad hauled them to the sawmill and the town of Millwood.

By 1890 Hiram Smith and A. D. Moore were, in their own estimation, "big-time operators." They were proud and vain, and anxious for the world to recognize that they were logging giant timber the way business giants would. They went East to sell their lumber and of course found buyers in New York and Chicago who would not believe such big trees existed.

"All right, gentlemen," the loggers said with open-handed gusto, "we invite you to Millwood—God's Country in the Sierra Nevada Mountains. You'll see many things you never saw before. And one of them is a pet pig that can do more tricks than a wagon-show clown!"

Some of the buyers came and their eyes were opened wide. Messrs. Smith and Moore entertained them with great barbecues of whole beeves and hogsheads of cider and harder liquors. The fun-and-frolic was giant-sized too, with dancing girls and field sports competing with the famed dancing pig from San Francisco's Kearney Street.

What the visitors saw in the green wonderland of high mountains and tall trees was an astounding sight of more than two thousand loggers, teamsters, sawmill hands—a bustling activity as fabulous in its way as the redwoods themselves. The Company town of Millwood boasted two hotels, a store, butcher and blacksmith shops, several doctors, boardinghouses and cookhouses. Smith and Moore exhibited their own beef cattle in pasture and in the slaughter pen they operated a mile from camp.

But their pride and joy was their flume, the water line that carried the sawed lumber down off the mountain to the railroad at Sanger. To prove what a wonder this was, visitors were invited to ride the fifty-four-mile length of it by special flume boat. Any who accepted were sorry they did. They never rode it twice.

When they cut the first trees in Converse Basin, Smith and Moore tried to haul the timber out by teams of twelve horses and mules. Trains of these wagons brought freight, machinery, and railroad iron up the narrow mountain roads and it seemed natural they should be used to take the lumber down. But the two bosses quickly saw this was too dangerous and antiquated a method for them. Too many wagon trains pitched down into the canyons trying to make dangerous, sharp turns.

"We'll build a flume," A. D. Moore announced with his customary smack of fist in palm, "a sort of water trough, like C. F. Ellsworth had up at Chico. It will be a big job and cost a pile of spondulix. But Hiram—we're going to do this thing right!"

Moore did not exaggerate. The flume cost a lot of "spondulix"—$300,000, which would have bought an entire logging operation with a thousand acres of timber anywhere in the West in 1885. But there seemed to be no shortage of funds and the men started the project by purchasing a small sawmill at Abbott Creek to cut ponderosa and sugar pine for the flume.

The construction took three years and was an engineering feat worthy of the Egyptian Pharaohs who built the pyramids. A man was killed for every mile of the elevated wooden ditch—and no wonder. Sometimes the workmen were suspended from cliffs, working on flimsy trestles sixty to eighty feet above rocky ledges, the boulder-studded canyon bottom five hundred feet below that.

The flume had sloping sides and a flat bottom. It was about four feet wide at the top. This was big enough to carry trains of lumber—bundles clamped together—or a narrow boat, called a "donkey," which conformed generally in shape to the sloping sides, in which two men could sit.

The water supply came from the reservoir behind the Sequoia Lake dam, which Smith and Moore had also built. The flow was rapid down to Millwood, where a slack grade reduced it to a gently moving stream. In the lumber yard here, men packed the boards in bundles measuring ten to twelve inches by eighteen to twenty feet. The bundles were strapped tight, then iron clamps were hooked over the butting ends and wedges driven to tighten the clamps. This insured the bundles and train against falling apart during the long and rough trip down.

Bundle after bundle was slipped into the slowly running stream, the herders hooking them together in trains of three and four bundles. They moved smoothly down the easy grades, went racing down cascading inclines, over eighty-five-foot trestles, along steep cliffs where the flume was anchored by cables to the overhanging rocks. South of Mill Flat Creek, past the lower sawmill, other bundles were hooked on.

At Rancheria Flat's Logging Camp No. 3, the next leveling-off stop, another train of three bundles was hooked on. They sailed on down to Kings River, reaching Camp No. 4½ at Cow Flat, where another three bundles were added to the train.

Nearing Maxon's Ranch, the flume came down sharply to cross the river on a high bridge. From here the wooden ditch was set on towering trestles paralleling the stream until it reached Centerville and turned westward into Sanger—the end of its fifty-four-mile run.

At certain points along the route of the flume, where the flow of water was slack, stations or camps were maintained—fifteen in all. From these stations, flume walkers patrolled the ditch on wooden catwalks attached to the flume's outside wall. These trouble shooters were constantly on guard to find lumber jams, breaks in the flume, or obstacles to the free passage of lumber trains. Looking down on steep mountain cliffs, deep ravines, and dangerous rocky canyons, the flume walkers or "flume snakes" made their way cautiously.

They carried picaroons—hand-fashioned in the company's blacksmith shop from double-bitted axes. One bit was only slightly reshaped, the other hammered to a curving point. When a lumber train buckled and blocked the stream, the flume walker reached out and hooked the bundles straight, starting them down again. As a train reached each of the several stations along the way, it was halted and held until the next train came along, then the two were hooked together. On the last miles of the journey, when the flume reached the valley floor, the trains flowing easily along might be composed of as many as

forty bundles of lumber. As they slipped into the yard at
Sanger they were broken apart, stacked for drying and
finishing. The flume had a capacity of 250,000 feet of
lumber a day.

A telephone service covered the entire fifty-four-mile
stretch. In case of accident or serious flume trouble, contact could be made with either terminal and with stations
along the way. One source of trouble was bad leaks or
water slopping over the rim on steep inclines. To re-
plenish the lost water, small streams were tapped by aux-
iliary flumes which were run into the main one.

The type of boat generally used was built with sloping
sides to conform to those of the flume, with a W or double
V bottom. This accommodated two men, the one ahead
bracing his feet against the blunt bow, the one behind
bracing his against the other man. There were no side
rails. The boats were used by Company inspectors, and
crews bringing supplies down from Millwood.

A ride down the flume was thrilling to the point of
being breath-stopping. Before starting a boat, a flag was
attached to a lumber train, signifying a boat was coming
next. No more lumber would be sent down until the flag
passed all stations and the "all clear" was telephoned back
to Millwood.

The boat was held back by the lumber herders while
the load was balanced heavily to stern. The two passengers
clambered in, and clutched the sides of the wobbly craft.
When it was released it shot on down, the riders praying
hard if they were not already shocked into a panic.

At times the boat would attain a speed of fifty miles an
hour and outrun the water, when it would scrape bottom

and come almost to a standstill. Then suddenly the water would catch up to the boat, shooting it ahead and cascading down on the passengers, perhaps washing their luggage or supplies over the side, even spilling the riders themselves into the wild water or down into canyon depths.

It was an ever-dangerous journey—not one taken by cautious people if they had a choice. But Smith and Moore were not in the business of supplying comfort to riders of the flume. It was part of their logging enterprise and it got most of the lumber out of the mountains.

Their bubble broke with typical Smith and Moore drama. One day their sawmill was cutting a hundred thousand feet of lumber. The next day it cut nothing—was shut down tightly. The wheels never turned again for the men who set them going. True to their flair for theatrics, Hiram C. Smith and A. D. Moore turned their backs on the Big Show they had staged for fifteen years and went back to San Francisco.

There was still timber to fell and manufacture and the two redwood kings eventually sold their interests to George Hume. They had ruled the destinies of two thousand people in producing lumber the hard, spectacular way. If it was going to be easy and dull from now on, "let George do it."

X

Washington . . . 1887

BIG STEEL ON PUGET SOUND

CAPTAIN William Renton listened to the scream of saws in the Port Blakely mill on Puget Sound, Washington. He could not see the big logs being fed to them or the tall masts of a sailing ship in the harbor. Captain Renton was blind, but he had a very clear picture of all the activity around the sawmill. It made him glad Sol Simpson and his family had arrived on this damp fall day of 1887.

He walked briskly between the lumber piles to the little office, outside which the newcomer stood with several other men. He counted something on the fingers of his rough hand, waited until the men spoke so he could determine where each stood.

"Mr. Simpson," he said, "we need you here. I am the manager of this mill and these gentlemen have put me at the head of a committee to get a railroad built. I have sent for you to build it. Are you ready to sign the contract?"

"Sure am, Captain Renton," was Sol Simpson's quick reply. "That's what I came clear up here for. Clear from Nevada."

Captain Renton shook his hand. "We need sixty mil-

102

lion feet of logs now and we want to grow. To do that we've got to haul our own logs. There are two railroads here now —the Mason County Central and the Satsop. They don't amount to too much but they're all the steel there is in this area and they dump logs in Puget Sound that are towed here to us and five other mills—Pope and Talbot at Port Gamble and Port Ludlow, St. Paul and Tacoma, the Port Discovery and Utsalady mills. To get more logs we've got to control more woods and haul our own."

He explained the situation at greater length and Sol G. Simpson lost no time in getting to work on his contract to build and operate the first major logging railroad on the Sound. He was a dynamo of energy, moving with a speed which had characterized his boyhood in Quebec, and his early youth in Nevada logging and lumbering. This was his first venture into railroad construction but he knew he could never haul logs or justify Captain Renton's faith in him if he stood still.

Boats began to arrive from Seattle and Tacoma with laborers and foremen, steel rails, tools, and equipment. This was a job to be done by hand-power and muscle— lots of it was needed to feed the hungry saws. The job became two jobs—one to build the docks at a point called New Kamilche, the other to slash the right-of-way west through virgin timber, great fir and cedar walls growing two and three hundred feet high out of junglelike tangles of underbrush. Thousands of these trees must be felled, big stumps blasted and torn from their age-old sockets in the earth.

Sol Simpson was a driver and his real helper was sweat. He made the woods ring with the sounds of double-bitted axes, the crashing of giant trees, the cracks of whips on the flanks of work horses that cleared away the logs and slash, the clank of steel sledges driving spikes to fasten down the rails on the rough-sawed ties.

Sol's three brothers—Joseph, George, and J. R.—worked in the crews. Sometimes his wife and two daughters—Irene Marie and Caroline—carried food and water to the men and acted as nurses when there were accidents. J. R. Simpson, known as "Bob," was lame and walked with a cane, but he was a popular foreman of the grade crews.

As the Puget Sound and Grays Harbor Railroad line drove through the timber it began to take on character and a new name—the Blakely—after the sawmill it was to be a part of. Logging camps opened up along the grade and bull teams brought logs to the landings ready for the first train to haul them to New Kamilche. As a railroad builder, Sol Simpson did not like bulls or oxen but since he was to operate the railroad when completed, which actually meant the whole logging operation for Captain Renton's sawmill, he wanted to get the logs out in the fastest, cheapest way. He watched the bulls work and talked to drivers like Billy Forbes and Orman Huntley.

For a sixteen-hour day driving, feeding, and looking after his charges, a good teamster got a hundred dollars a month. On Sundays he had to fit the bulls with shoes, cut their horns to stumps, and clamp brass caps over the ends.

The skid roads were about a mile long, studded with short logs laid eight to ten feet apart. A six-yoke team of bulls could make four turns or trips daily with logs twenty-four feet long—ten to twelve thousand board-feet. Sol

Simpson thought this daily production could be doubled by using horses. He said nothing about it and did nothing while the railroad was a-building. But he was ready.

The day came when the last spike was driven and out of the roundhouse at Matlock churned Engine No. 1. With a string of short trucks she steamed up to the wood pile, loaded her tender, and went slowly downgrade for the first load of logs. The crew christened her the Blizzard. In subsequent months other engines followed—geared locomotives for the steeper grades and to haul logs between the rails, dragged over the ties. They kept the wood bucks slaving, sawing and splitting prime wood for the insatiable boilers. More and more men were hired, more crews added. The Blakely was booming.

And as it prospered the small feeder railroads nearby went into disuse, the rails turning to rust. The Satsop Railroad had used up most of its capital in financing a sawmill in Tacoma. The banks took possession of it. The Mason County Central was also in bad condition and soon went bankrupt. All this meant more work for the Blakely.

"But," the woodsmen began to say, "something's gone wrong with Sol Simpson. He's good at building railroads but what he don't know about logging would fill a hollow tree. What's he getting rid of all those bulls for? You can't log with horses. He won't last out the year!"

But that was what Sol G. Simpson was doing—logging with the finest and strongest horses he could find. He had eighty of them working in teams of ten and twelve. They were big horses, weighing from seventeen to nineteen hundred pounds each, some of them costing as much as five hundred dollars. Logger Simpson did not mind the gloomy predictions. He bought more horses and along the railroad grade he established a farm to grow hay, turnips, and carrots—fine fare for working animals.

And now he had another surprise for the men, something other loggers said would work better than bulls and horses. A barge arrived one day with a Dolbeer donkey engine, invented by John Dolbeer of Eureka, California, another lumberman who had grown impatient with animals on the skid road. The engine was crude but effective. Its boiler was vertical and the single-cylinder vertical engine powered an upright capstan or spool around which went the manila and wire rope. Breakdowns were frequent but Sol Simpson found the Dolbeer donkey good enough for a start. He bought several more and they snorted a steamy good-by to animal power on the Blakely.

These years also marked the beginning of expansion for the Simpson effort. A new man had appeared on the scene who at once showed signs of leadership. A. H. Anderson had been busy putting new life into the Satsop Railroad and had opened up several logging camps. Now he and logger Simpson joined forces, forming the Simpson Logging Company and the Peninsular Railroad.

Then the day in 1898 came when the steamer *Portland* docked at Seattle with a million dollars in gold dust and wild-talking passengers running down the gangplank. Gold had been discovered in Alaska. When the news was spread by telegraph and word-of-mouth, the rush to the Klondike was on, coming to a head in 1898. The stampede of men north took its toll of the Simpson camps and log production suffered. But not for long. The bedraggled, disappointed loggers returned after a few months, glad to be back to work and a life they knew something about.

Sol Simpson and A. H. Anderson now purchased the Silvia Mill Company at Montesano, moved it close to Shelton, and they were in the cedar shingle business. With Mark Reed, the two organized the Phoenix Logging Company to cut timber on Hood Canal. In 1900, Sol Simpson and C. D. Lane formed the White Star Steamship Company and put three steamers on the run from Seattle to Nome, Alaska.

Logging in the Simpson camps was going at top speed in spite of forest fires, snow drifts, a wind storm which crashed a big tree down on a locomotive. One hundred and sixty million feet of logs were dumped into Puget Sound, and, in 1898, a forty-two-ton locomotive was added to the Simpson rolling stock. The company now had eighty miles of tracks on two lines.

The "rugged fir," Sol G. Simpson, died in 1906, having left a thriving memorial in the Simpson Logging Company which continued to expand and prosper. Its founder was one of logging history's greats—a man with ambition, inventive genius, and the same geared drive that sent his logging locomotives grinding up steep forest grades.

XI

Washington . . . 1890

"HUMP! YOU—BUCK!"

How to get the logs to the mill? That was always the big question in Western logging. To fell the trees and buck them into movable lengths was the easiest job. All that was needed was muscle, axes, and saws. But then the logs must be taken out of the woods.

The simplest way to move them was by river—if there was one handy. Build the sawmill downstream and let the current carry the logs to it. But they still had to be hauled to the river. The fir, cedar, and spruce logs cut in the West were of great size, far bigger than any trees cut in the eastern United States. Six to twelve feet was the average diameter. And the redwoods were bigger than that.

In the early days the only known method of moving such giant-sized logs was by means of giant-sized animals— bulls weighing up to 1,800 pounds. Horses were used to some extent but usually proved inadequate. The huge bulls had tremendous pulling power and when used in teams of four to eight yoke, or eight to sixteen animals, they could drag the big chunks of trees down the skid roads with dogged force and unending endurance. They could, that is, if the drivers—sometimes called "skinners" and "whackers"—were as good as C. W. "Cy" Blackwell.

This famous logger and bull driver came from Maine in 1873 to drive teams of horses in the early settling of California and in logging pine on the Truckee River. Then he took up the handling of oxen for logging purposes and drove them in the Coos Bay fir and spruce region of Oregon. Working north he became one of the pioneer timbermen of Grays Harbor on the Washington coast, an area which held one of the greatest stands of timber ever known.

Here comes a bull team now—and that deep-throated, booming voice could be none other than Cy Blackwell's. The two lead bulls, like the others behind them, are yoked together at their thick necks by a heavy wood-and-leather frame, their horns are capped with brass knobs, and they swing their heads from side to side with each plodding step. Four more pairs of them follow, lashing their tails at the big blue-bellied flies and darting hornets.

The last two bulls are the wheelers. Running back between the ten grunting, sweating beasts is a heavy chain linked to an iron dog driven in the lead log. And there by the near wheeler strides Cy Blackwell, steel-shod goad stick in his hand, ready to be jabbed into the thick hide of any bull that lags or stumbles.

"Hump! You—Buck! Git on—Brin—Star!" he bellows, as the animals jerk and sway. "Hi-e-ee—Hank! Ye-ow-ow! You—Mig!"

Now, out of the billowing cloud of dust, the skid greaser comes into view—a youngster in a torn shirt, but still a logger, at his first job in the woods. He swings a ten-pound can of black grease and dashes in behind the pounding hooves of the wheelers, just ahead of the lead log, swabbing the slippery substance on the small, half-buried cross logs of the skid road.

Cy Blackwell squints at the logs bumping and sliding along, sees one bull slip to a knee, goads him on, spits dirt out of his mouth and shouts the team on to greater effort at a slight curve in the skid road. The swamper runs up on the far side of the load, which is six logs chained one behind the other, and daubs more grease on the skids. The tall bull skinner bawls out another command. The beasts groan and grunt. But in ten minutes now this turn of logs will come to a stop at the end of the road. More timber at the river.

Cy Blackwell had his own idea about getting the logs out. He built a "splash" dam on the Hoquiam River—the first in Grays Harbor. His theory was to trap water in the river until the "pond" created was filled with logs, then open the dam to let the sudden flood carry the logs downstream over the eddies and shallows.

Other loggers laughed and said such a harebrained idea was a joke. It was such a joke that it worked and dozens more splash dams were built by loggers in the area—on the Queets, Wishkah, and Humptulips rivers. It was said Cy Blackwell saved the Grays Harbor loggers many millions of dollars, since splash dams delayed the construction of expensive railways.

Blackwell and every other good bull whacker earned $100 to $150 "a month and found," the loggers' term for bed and board. He worked sixteen hours a day and nursed his charges like stubborn children from four o'clock in the morning until he pounded on the last shoe and slapped their rumps at ten. He became such a part of the bulls' lives that his clothes took on the animals' aroma. This went unnoticed only in the saloons, which had a pungent smell of their own.

It was here the drivers did their gossiping and boasting. When two or more of them gathered in the sawdust-floored drink emporiums, one at least was sure to speak boldly of his animals.

"You say your team is trained good? By the Pillar of Paul, I got bulls that'll pull anything that's loose—and a lot of what ain't. Give them critters good footing and they'll draw the meanness right out of a stump!"

Logging bulls were housed in barns or covered corrals at the woods camp. They ate hay and barley and were occasionally washed down. The blacksmith usually had his forge here or handy for heating the shoes, bending steel straps for the yokes, and linking up the heavy bull chains.

The bull whacker acted as veterinarian whenever oxen were hurt. They were never sick and were bothered only by the pesky flies and stinging hornets. But they did break legs and sprain ankles when their massive weight fell sideways suddenly or lead logs jumped ahead and crashed into their hoofs. And Cy Blackwell was as good a man with splints and arnica as any animal doctor. Because he was a top driver with respect for the bulls, fewer accidents happened to his teams.

He would scoff at the antics of some young, daredevil skinners. A few were deliberately cruel or wanted to be spectacular and attract the foreman's attention to them—showing him how rough and effective they were in getting work out of the animals. Blackwell would watch a man trying to start a balky bull team after the turn of logs had "hung up" or snagged to a stop. The man would swear to the treetops, jump up on the back of a bull, prance and dig his heels into the creature's back as he roared and cajoled. Cy would turn away in disgust, knowing such brutal attacks would not drive bulls into action. He believed in being firm, even rough, and yet kind, too. He said a good bull driver always kept his animals in fear of the authority of the commands, rather than in fear of the driver.

A big part of the bull skinner's job was getting along with his fellow loggers. He needed the help of the hook tender especially. This man made up the turns or trains of logs. Once they were sniped—the front edges of the cut beveled so they would not catch on the road skids, the hook tender showed his helper where to drive the dogs and chains to link the logs together. Both of them followed the turn down the skid road, taking care of any hangups. At the landing by the mill or river bank, they removed the dogs and chains, throwing them over the yokes to be carried back to the woods where more logs waited.

And then it was Cy Blackwell's time to get the bulls ready for another battle with fifty tons of cranky timber. He sighted back along the logs—a foot between the ends of each, the lead log with bark stripped off.

He watched the bulls chewing their cuds in lethargic repose, seemingly asleep on their feet except for the deliberate movement of their jaws. He hooked the butt chain into the ring on the front set of dogs—and whistled. Chains rattled as the bulls stirred restlessly. In low tones he spoke to the near wheeler.

"Ready to move, Jay. Keep that Ham in line now."

Both wheelers heard their names and lifted feet as

though in response. That slight action set the other animals alert, jaws ceasing to grind. Cy moved up to the second pair.

"Hi-yo! Hank—Brin. You—Star. Git—up, Bright. You—Hank!"

The bulls lunged, pawed, jerked, shoulders thrust into the yokes—but all out of rhythm. Chains rattled and shook but the logs remained solid to the skids. Blackwell spat in the dust and sighed. Momentarily the oxen ceased their straining, sank back, warily eyeing the master creature at their side with his stick going *tap-tap-tap.* Cy waited only until the team was settled, then again roared:

"By all the holy hollyhocks! Up—Ham—Bright—Star! Hi-yo! Yo-yo! Ham—Brin! Git—up. Ye-ow-ow!"

At this frightful bellow, the bulls snorted, tensed, and staggered forward. One of them lay back, another made no move. The goad descended on them with more awe-inspiring invective. The steel spur dug into the thick hides, paining the animals into life. Another explosion of words followed. A solid whack on a rump. A thrumming of tightened chains.

Cy swept his dusty eye along the double row of bulls, saw their muscles bulging in strain. Now he unleashed another roar. Yokes squealed, shoulders lunged, front hoofs pawed, rear ones dug. The butt log trembled and screeched, wood against wood. It moved ahead—and then the second stirred. Blackwell was ripping out commands again and his bulls were pulling, heaving mightily. Finally the rear log of the turn jerked forward.

Cy Blackwell's last turn of the day was headed for the river.

XII

Oregon . . . 1893

THE GREAT SUGAR PINE CHUTE

"You say the logs slide down a mile a minute?"

The banker was skeptical. He had come to the sawmill town of Klamathon on the Klamath River in southern Oregon because logger John Cook wanted to borrow money. Now he listened with curiosity to Cook's description of his Klamathon chute.

"I said over a mile a minute," repeated the tall, bearded man with worry lines deep in his weathered face. "And what I mean is, a mile and a half a minute. Sometimes of a frosty morning, those logs scoot down that chute so fast they smoke. Mister—you don't look like you believe a thing I say."

"Oh, I do, Mr. Cook," the man insisted. "Indeed I do. But this is very hard for me to grasp."

"Well, I'm not a loose-talking man. The logs that chute is built of are all hand-hewn smooth and about halfway down they're all charred from heat. Sometimes those logs hit the river so fast they bounce clean over to the other bank and we got to go haul them back in the water."

The banker wanted to believe. His bank had money to help advance worthy businesses and he had been told what a good risk John Cook was. An upright, courageous man, he had come from Michigan to this Black Mountain region of Oregon in 1891 and bought 27,000 acres of timberland, starting a new industry where an earlier one had failed. High water had broken through a dam in the river and washed out a partly built sawmill, blacksmith shop, and the town of Klamath City which was called Pokegama by the Indians.

John Cook had new ideas, people said. He had demonstrated it by rebuilding the dam, completing the sawmill and box factory and helping develop the settlement's two hotels, boardinghouses, stores, livery stable, school, churches, and lodge hall.

"Sure, Mr. Cook—I believe you," the visitor said emphatically, "but is the chute greased? Why do the logs go down so fast?"

"Greased?" The big man guffawed so loudly the sound rolled over the bare river banks. "Grease costs money. You're a man who can understand that. Besides, the problem we got is not to make the logs go fast but to slow them up. We got diamond spikes at the bottom of the chute to keep 'em from shooting clear into Californy."

The banker seemed embarrassed. He thought John Cook was clearly exaggerating. The look on his face said as much. But he would be tolerant, accepting the owner's words as evidence of pride. "Well, Mr. Cook," he said. "When can I see all this for myself?"

"Right soon. After dinner we're taking a team up in the hills to where we're logging. You'll get an eyeful. And I hope I get a hatful—of greenbacks."

On the way upriver in the buckboard, the logger let the span of sorrels take easy strides up the steep grades as

he flung a hand out over the river. "The miners get gold
out of the sand down there. They trap the silt in wing
dams and give our river drivers trouble. You see, after
we get the logs in the water, we have to drive them down
to where we've built cribs filled with rocks. From there
an endless chain carries them into the sawmill."

When the rig reached the top of the first bald hill the
two men could see in the distance the low dark bulk of
the timber stretching across the horizon. They rode on in
the hot sun watching the horses toil up the grade tossing
their manes and tails at the constant attacks of flies and
hornets.

In an hour they had reached the area of scrub timber
—lodge pole and jack and yellow pine—and progressing
along the dusty wheel tracks between the trees, the air
cooled and the shade of bigger trees began. Suddenly the
light wagon dropped into a gully and the logger pulled
up on the reins.

Thundering up the foot-deep dust on the far side of
the draw, in a cloud of fuss and fury, was a four-horse
team pulling a great pair of wooden wheels. Suspended
between them, its rear end dragging and sending up billows of dust, was a big log covered with orange and black
bark. The driver rode the left wheel horse, holding lines
on the two leaders and putting all his rough heartiness
into the voice which urged the horses to dig and pull.

"Yah, Mike! Louie! Bear down—you lazy alligators!
Yah—buck 'er up!"

The voice roared, sixteen hoofs pounded and pawed,
the log bounced, and the long wooden tongue jerked.
John Cook slapped his legs as though to help the horses

and when the load had finally reached the crest of the hill and the dust settled, he shook the reins and the buckboard moved ahead.

"That's sugar pine and that's the way we get our logs out of the woods. Big wheels—some stinger-tongue and some slip-tongue which are better. We got twenty rigs like that carrying logs to the chute head."

"How big are those wheels, Mr. Cook?"

"Twelve feet high, those were. Some are ten. Some are wood and some are iron—made down in Redding. Cost a sight too—but not so much as that railroad we're building to run a real locomotive on. Old Blue's her name. Narrow gauge. The first steam logging lokey in Klamath County. We're bringing her up from the south now with a team of eight bulls."

They stopped again to watch another crew chaining two logs to a second pair of high wheels. One man had dug a shallow trench under the logs. A chain was pushed through it and when the wheels were backed astride the logs, they were secured to the axle. "Hip!" shouted the loader and the horses lunged ahead, the tongue sliding forward and pulling on the chain which lifted the front end of the logs from the ground. The driver mounted his wheeler and gave his own shout to the horses, the load moving slowly ahead.

"The harder those critters pull," the logger said, "the higher the logs will hang. And the other way around. When the team comes to a stop down grade, the logs drop and drag—acting like a brake. Only when they don't, they smash the horses' hind feet. Get on there, Bessie. Mister—we'll go to camp and then on down to the landing. Then you'll really see something that will make your eyes pop."

The camp was not much more than a collection of shanties, the larger one being the cookhouse. Beyond it were the barn and blacksmith shop and around them a clutter of high wheels and heavy wagons. Men were gathered around the forge and shed, where horses were being shod.

"We call this place Snow. Plenty of it come winter."

John Cook drove close to the men and tossed out the sack of mail he had brought from town. "Supply wagon will be up before supper," he told the group and headed the horses down into a shallow ravine where another crew was building railroad track. He pointed to the piles of gravel and rail iron.

"In thirty days we'll be hauling logs to the chute by train so the horses won't have such a long haul and they can get more logs in. There's no end of timber to cut but horses and manpower are costly, and scarce. Once we get Old Blue steaming over the grades we'll double our production. Yonder's the log landing. Chute's ahead there —on the high point."

The banker saw only a level platform built of logs on which others were stacked as they came from the high wheels. Men crow-hopped over the deck prying the newly cut logs along with cant hooks, calling out:

"Heave ho! Bend her in there, Ben. You—Joe. Throw a sag into her. Ready now—heave!"

The great bulks rolled ahead slowly. At the lower level of the deck a cable was looped and hooked around the foremost log. A hand was raised in signal and off to one side a donkey engine snorted, blowing steam as the cable snapped taut and the log jerked forward.

They were now being lined up one behind another in a trough at the far edge of the deck. Beyond that was open sky and faraway hills. John Cook beckoned his visitor along behind a moving log and they stood at the chute head, high on a hill which overlooked a curving stretch of the Klamath River on the Oregon-California border.

The banker, an intelligent man, was instantly amazed at the engineering feat the sight represented. A channel had been cut in the rock of the hillside and logs, hewn flat, lined the sides and bottom of the cut—large logs at the sides and small ones on the bottom, all worn as smooth as glass. Down the steep slope and clear to the river bank the chute extended like a great, long scratch some giant had made in the rock and sand. Halfway down the chute, logs rested on a trestle and then entered another cleft in the rock.

"Clear back!"

The shout behind him made the viewer jump. His guide pulled him to one side and up on a hummock. A train of logs was lined up at the brink of the chute, held back by an iron bar wedged into the rock by a bearlike man who kept his eyes on something far down below. John Cook pointed.

"Watch there—at the far end of the chute."

A white flag appeared—a tiny patch held aloft and then dropped. The chute tender yanked the iron bar aside and the first big sugar-pine log shuddered into a slow downward motion. A hundred feet on, it seemed to leap ahead and was streaking down, squealing wood-against-wood, plunging headlong through the rock cut and over the trestle.

The banker stood fascinated, his eyes following the ten-ton missile as it shot through the second rock cut and out into the open again. It seemed only a few seconds until it reached the lower end of the chute and struck the water with a great fan-shaped spray that showered the trees on the opposite side of the river.

"That's an amazing sight!" he marveled. "Astounding!"

"Beats all, don't it?" was John Cook's laconic comment.

Another log and then another went streaking down the chute until all were dropped, each making the peacock-tail splash in the river. There they remained, floating like tired animals in the backwash of the stream, and men the size of ants were jumping from one to another, herding them into the shallows. The logger was pointing again.

"Look close at that chute a third of the way down. See all that black part of the wood? That's burned—friction from the logs going down so fast. You can't see the smoke from it except on cold mornings. The chute is twenty-six hundred and fifty feet long and the logs drop eight hundred and thirty-four feet. It takes about eighteen seconds for a log to start and then hit the river. Sometimes the water pressure splits a log. When it's frosty they go faster and we drive spikes in the bottom end to slow them up."

John Cook turned away—back to his troubles. He had many—too many. There were continual fights on the river between the log drivers and the miners, some of them resulting in doctors' bills and property damage costs. And he could not declare open war on the mining interests because their placer operations downriver offered Cook and Company an outlet for many thousands of dollars' worth of lumber.

Another trouble was the risky rafting of lumber downstream from the sawmill. The last expedition had broken up and most of the lumber was lost. Rafts of about ten thousand feet were made up at the mill, the boards chained together to make the whole unit float like a barge, about five feet showing above the water line. Four men with long sweeps kept the craft from going on the rocks or grounding on the banks where the river curved. If all went well for the first few miles there were the dangerous rocks at Lime Gulch and Humbug Creek. That was where the last wreck had occurred, the raft men being lucky to get ashore with their lives.

And now there was the tragedy on one of the log drives. John Cook took from his jacket pocket a newspaper clipping, torn from a page of the Klamath Falls *Express.*

Three men were drowned [he read for the tenth time], on the Klamath River the 19th of this month. The accident happened about 3 o'clock in the afternoon on what is known as Hessig's Bar, a mile northeast of Shovel Creek. The dam at Chase's had been closed down the night previous, and while the water was low, blasting operations had been carried on to break the jam. When the flood came the crew jumped in with peavies and rolled the logs into the current.

Directly below the jam a whirlpool had formed in the deep water, and George Marsh the foreman, saw his crew of twenty-four men were in danger of losing their lives, if the logs should begin to move. Marsh called the men back to shore and all obeyed

except four—Dan Shea, Leslie Shrieves, Andy Davidson and a man named Donnelly, all courageous log
drivers. When the jam started the three former men
jumped into the water. Shea and Shrieves were never
seen again. Donnelly was carried into the whirlpool
and rose to the surface, calling frantically for help.
None was given him or could be given him. Davidson
in the meantime had clung to a log and passed
through the whirlpool to safety.

The big logger shook his head sorrowfully. He knew
all these facts only too well and knew something would
have to be done for the families of the lost men. It was
all part of his need for more working capital. When he
walked back to the banker he spoke of all the things he
could do with a hundred thousand dollars—and his appeal
bore fruit. On the return drive to town, his passenger
agreed to approve the loan.

But John Cook was to know many more money difficulties and tragedies before the big one which marked
the end of his Klamath River operations. On Monday,
October 13, 1902, fire broke out in the Klamathon settlement and a strong west wind rapidly spread the flames.
Eight million feet of lumber, the two box factories, the
sawmill, and some thirty homes—all became piles of
smoking ashes in a loss of $500,000.

Cook and Company was wiped out and nothing of
Klamathon was left but the memory of logs sliding down-
hill "like greased lightning" and of John Cook—one of
Western logging history's great men, admired for his
energy, daring, and human understanding.

XIII

Oregon . . . 1905

THE CLEAN GUY

SOME of W. F. Jewett's men thought he was a hardhearted slave driver. Some knew he was. Still others, and this included the wives in "Spotless Town," thought the big boss was as fine a man as ever settled on the Oregon coast. Who else would send back to Maine for barrels of clams and plant them in the tidelands for his employees' benefit? Yet whatever else they considered Mr. Jewett to be, everybody agreed "he was sure a man to keep things clean."

This trait alone was enough to make the sawmill settlement of Gardiner, Oregon, and the logging woods back of it, different. Most West Coast lumber towns were dirty —smudgy and unkempt from wood smoke and the natural shoddiness of short-term workers. If a supply clerk found the item "Paint" on his buying list, he assumed it was a mistake and drew a pencil mark through it.

But Gardiner was clean. Sailors on schooners entering Winchester Bay at the mouth of the Umpqua River saw a hillside dotted with pretty cottages all painted white. Then they saw the company store, machinery sheds, and the paddle-wheel steamer *Eva*. They also were painted white. And all this gave the place the name "White City-by-the-Sea."

W. F. Jewett had learned cleanliness in Maine—the cleanliness of body, home, and soul. As a boy he had been disciplined to keep himself and everything around him spotless, was trained in the belief that this was the clear path to Heaven. He always heard his mother's voice telling him, "Cleanliness is next to Godliness." He brought this belief with him to Oregon in 1877 and it dominated his reign as manager of the Gardiner Lumber Company for forty years. He tried to instill a sense of cleanliness in everybody from his daughter Narcissa and son William to the lowliest whistle punk in the logging crews and the newest man on the sawmill green chain.

Manager Jewett had other qualities which matched this obsession. He had a New England conscience, hated idleness and any appearance of it. He was also a teetotaler. When he stepped off the ship at the Gardiner wharf to take over the lumbering business, he saw a millhand leave the store with a bottle of whisky.

"How does that happen?" he asked George Hinsdale, one of the owners with Ed Breen and J. B. Leeds. The question puzzled Hinsdale.

"Why, he bought it I guess."

"Your store sells liquor?"

"Of course. Why not? Booze and boards go together, don't they? How can you get men to work hard getting out logs and lumber without it?"

Jewett stared at him uncompromisingly. "I'll show you."

He did. From that day alcoholic drinks were never sold

in the Gardiner store. There were many complaints and a few disgruntled men quit but they were replaced by steadier workers. In a year George Hinsdale was forced to admit the dry operation was getting out more logs and lumber by far than the wet one had. And there were fewer fights and less labor trouble.

With his other State of Maine habits, "the clean guy" had a deep sense of thrift. Almost any day he would round up three or four boys and jingle some coins in front of their big eyes.

"Joe—Heber—Willie, you can buy a lot of licorice sticks and rock candy with these. Saul, you're the trimmerman's boy, aren't you? Now—you see that skiff down there in the river? Can you row it? Well, take that skiff around the shoreline of the bay and you'll find a lot of logs that have drifted downriver from the woods. Bring them in to the boom man at the mill. I'll pay you boys fifty cents a log. Hop to it now. I don't want you boys loafing around and getting into trouble. That costs me money."

Jewett had also an abiding love for ships and river boats. He gloried in navigating the Umpqua River and Winchester Bay in the *Restless* and *Eva*—both wood-burning stern-wheelers that carried passengers and freight to Scottsburg, thirty miles upstream. He saw to it the company acquired an interest in these two, as well as the *O. B. Hinsdale* and the lumber cargo schooners *Lily, Lucy,* and *Beulah*. While any of these ships were loading he would be crowding the tallyman's elbow or checking the stays with the skippers. But he was not always on hand when some ship arrived without advance notice.

One gloomy day the three-masted bark *Palmerston* made

port. She had sailed in ballast from San Francisco with one passenger, her charter owner. This pompous gentleman came down the gangplank and at once demanded to see Mr. Jewett. He wanted eighty thousand feet of spruce and he wanted it loaded at once. Storekeeper Louis Seymour smiled at the man's officiousness.

"Expect Mr. Jewett is up in the woods," he explained. "He generally is, every day. A hard-working man he is, sir."

The lumber buyer stormed and slapped the ends of the flour barrels. "Well—get me a man to take me to him! My charter only lasts forty days and twelve of it's gone already. How far is this logging camp?"

The storekeeper was anxious enough to pacify a man who was eager to buy over a thousand dollars' worth of lumber. He left the store to find someone to run the hand speeder up the railroad to camp. His eye roved from the dock to the hillside covered with the white painted homes of the married sawmill workers. An old horse was drawing a wood wagon down a lane between the houses. Ahead of it walked a forlorn-looking man in somber black oilskins. At every few steps he would stoop, pick up refuse or paper, and throw it in the wagon.

"There's Mr. Jewett," Louis Seymour said.

"Where?" asked the buyer. The storekeeper pointed.

The stranger was astounded. "You mean that disreputable old trash picker is the man I've come clear from San Francisco to buy lumber from?"

"Guess it is," answered the storekeeper. "Anyway, it's W. F. Jewett. He likes to keep things clean."

He stepped to the side of the store building and struck

a ship's bell. The resounding tones brought the manager's head up, as this was the signal to summon him for any emergency. And when the trash collector came down the hill and shed his oilskins in the office, shook hands, and spoke a spare half-dozen crisp words, the lumber buyer began shedding some of his own sense of importance. When the *Palmerston* sailed, he was well satisfied with his deal and knew he had met a sound businessman—even if he did have a hobby of picking up odds and ends in the road.

In March, 1905, the trouble began with one Sven Lindquist and it left W. F. Jewett with an injury to his spirit from which he never recovered. It may even have influenced his final physical illness several years later. The belief that a man could be vindictive to such a degree shocked him deeply.

The company store was the only place in Gardiner where men could yarn and pass along gossip. After supper on winter nights they milled around the boiler-plate stove that burned four-foot slabs and talked about everything from the raw deal the Oregon politicians were putting over to the price of Star chewing tobacco. And one who made the most noise this raw, blustery March night was Sven Lindquist, a general handyman in the woods. He had been a hook tender but had become undependable for a regular job. Logging boss Wilson was "just keeping him around."

After a hot argument with the sawmill edgerman during which Sven had worked himself into a violent state, someone in the crowd scooped up a handful of sawdust from the floor and flung it in the Swede's face with a shout: "Go crawl back under a board and shut up!"

The logger went berserk, grabbing one jug of cider after another from the row on the counter and hurling them against the wall. Work clothes, open barrels of crackers, and corn meal were showered and ruined by broken glass and apple juice. Then Lindquist grabbed a steel-shod pike pole and brandished it, defying the crowd. His eyes were blazing and his lips almost foaming in a mad-dog frenzy.

"You fallas stay avay!" he croaked at his imagined tormentors. "Ay poke holes in anybody's head. Yah! Ay fix you all tam stumble bums. Good Ay fix you—and Mister Yewett too—by yumping Yee!"

Boss Jewett had been told of the ruckus and was hurrying down from his home. He knew the trouble maker well, having shaken him by the neck more than once trying to get him to work. By the time he arrived at the store, Sven was gone and the men were chuckling over the antics of "that crazy Swede." Jewett was horrified, shaking his head at the messy debris the man had created, and he set about at once to clean it up. The loungers knew logger Lindquist was in for a good cross-hauling.

But they were mistaken. Bright and early as usual W. F. Jewett appeared in the woods and asked Sam Wilson where Lindquist was.

"Well, he ain't," said the bull of the woods. "And I hope that wall-eyed maggot don't show up again. Keep him out of here, Jewett, before I or somebody heaves a chain block at him!"

This seemed unlikely to happen as Sven Lindquist had

Admiralty Hall—Cyrus Walker's castle.

ABOVE: Even Smith and Moore's bulls were bigger—to match the biggest redwoods of them all. *(Page 94)*. BELOW: "They had special augers forged in Redding—ten and twelve feet long"—to bore holes for blasting the big logs. *(Page 95)*.

"... to slash the right-of-way west through virgin timber ..." *(Page 103)*.

ABOVE: "At this frightful bellow, the bulls snorted, tensed, and staggered forward." *(Page 113)*. BELOW: "The clean guy" loved ships, like this lumber schooner sailing off the Oregon coast.

". . . a veritable whale of a log raft." *(Page 133)*.

"Up out of the tangle came the log, threshing and slapping like something alive . . ." *(Page 165)*.

ABOVE: The high climber begins his ascent to the towering crown. *(Page 173)*. RIGHT: "The big green crown had snapped free and was hurtling earthward . . ." *(Page 175)*.

"Tracks to the clouds." No engineering feat was more spectacular than the incline railroad. *(Page 180)*.

disappeared completely. A parcel of boys was set out to
search the woods and every shed and shanty where the
man might be hiding. There was no ship at the wharf,
only the paddle boat *Eva* at the river slip, the *Restless*
being at Scottsburg. The *Eva*'s skipper, Neil Cornwall,
had steam up but curiously no one had seen him or the
mate all day.

In the stormy darkness that night they found out why.
George Sutcliff, the *Eva*'s eighteen-year-old fireman, came
stumbling up to the Jewett home. He was out of breath,
coatless, shivering from cold and fright. He pointed to
one shoe. The toe of it had been sliced off cleanly and
George's toes protruded.

"Mr. Jewett—he—that Sven Lindquist—he's gonna blow
her up! The *Eva*. He's there—with an ax. The boiler's
about ready to bust!"

Young Sutcliff was in a state of near collapse but rallied
as he realized that he was free from the ordeal on the boat.
Jewett pieced together the blurted-out fragments of the
story.

Sven Lindquist had slept on the boat the night before,
had surprised Cornwall and the mate in their berths and
bound and gagged them. When the young fireman appeared for work, the crazed Swede had stood over him
with an ax in one hand, the skipper's deer rifle in the
other, and forced him to stoke the boiler.

All day George had cut wood and fed the gluttonous
firebox under threats of sudden death. Lindquist had
shot out the steam gauge and closed all safety valves.
When the steam did not go up fast enough, he attacked
the fireman with the ax. Now, tonight, with the gun

pointed at his head, he had sent George to get kerosene
out of the back room of the store and the boy had fled
for help.

As he listened, Jewett was pulling on his jacket. With
George Sutcliff at his heels he went for Si Gillan, the
green chain foreman, who acted as the only policeman
the community had. Gillan was dedicated to peace and
harmony but willing to back up his authority with his
fists or a gun. Jewett was unarmed, yet fearless. He shook
his head in disbelief of all he had heard.

"They call Gardiner 'White City.' How can it be if
we let this sort of thing go on?"

As the trio approached the river boat, shots were heard
all too clearly. Then there were sounds of glass breaking,
dull thuds, the sharp cracking and splintering of wood—
all of which sent shudders through the mill manager.
Through the *Eva*'s square cabin windows it looked as
though a typhoon had struck. The rich, dark paneling had been hacked into strips, lamps jerked from
their brackets, crockery smashed, furniture upended and
broken. While Jewett stood shocked into apathy, Si Gillan
crept to the window of the captain's cabin and smashed
the glass. Crawling in, he found Neil Cornwall strapped
helplessly to his bunk.

He was released and the two slipped along the upper
deck, motioning to Jewett to stay on the dock. But "the
clean guy" could not. A devil had made a shambles of
his pride and joy and not he or any other power could
have held him back. He walked boldly up the gangplank
and across the foredeck, and lowered himself through the
companionway to the engine room.

Sven Lindquist had been impatiently waiting for the boy fireman and the kerosene. Now he saw a tall man, dressed as carelessly as any camp swamper, slowly descending the ladder. He also saw no fear in the man's chalk-colored face, only utter disbelief. The boiler room, its wood bin empty, was in almost as sad a state as the cabin. Steam was escaping from pipes bent at all angles, the steam gauge was nicked and torn with bullet holes and canted to one side, the remains of stateroom chairs and wooden fittings lay on the floor ready to be fed to the fire.

With an unfaltering step W. F. Jewett walked slowly up to the wild-eyed desecrator. Lindquist now seemed to be in a trance. He made no move toward resistance until the manager laid hold on the rifle. Then he seemed to fly apart, jumping up and down like a child in a tantrum, shrieking:

"Go avay! Go avay! You no good running tis place. Ay know you. Ay run it better. Ay have boat to sail home to Stockholm!"

And then after another burst of stark invective, Sven Lindquist folded into a limp bundle in front of the fire-box door. The one-man mutiny had ended. When the *Eva*'s captain and the green chain foreman appeared, W. F. Jewett handed them the rifle and moved silently away. Cornwall and Gillan carried the unconscious body up the companionway and saw their big boss pacing the storm-swept deck. He turned to them.

"Don't injure the poor man, Si. He's not to blame. Completely out of his mind. We must watch him carefully. Guard him, by all means. There will be a ship in here within a week and we will have him taken to a hospital in Portland or Astoria."

"The *Eva* is a terrible wreck," her skipper lamented.

"So am I, Neil," Jewett replied. "I've taken one of the worst blows of my life. I never outgrew my love for ships. But we'll repair her as good as new. I feel very sorry for that poor demented man."

The *Eva* was restored when paneling could be brought from the Philippines. She made many more stern-wheel voyages up and down the Umpqua. But before many years W. F. Jewett took to a wheel chair. From it he operated the Gardiner enterprise but no longer could he be in the woods by breakfast time—or pick paper scraps off the dirt lanes of "White City-by-the-Sea."

XIV

Oregon . . . 1906

WHEN FORESTS WENT TO SEA

T HE fisherman tied his boat and came running up the Astoria dock. "I seen a vale!" he panted, wild-eyed. "Right off Sontag Point—a vale bigger as tat cannery building—long as tis dock It was chasing two tugboats down ta river!"

The loungers haw-hawed their derision. "Too much aquavit for you, Arne. Whoever heard of a whale in the Columbia River?"

"Val, I did," the sturdy Finn insisted. "Vit my own two eyes I seen tat vale. Going so slow maybe but a big humpbacked fellow with stripes around him!"

Nobody believed Arne for all his reputation as a hard-working, trustworthy man. But his story was investigated and when the truth of it became known the Astoria, Oregon, Finns let out many a chuckle in the steam of their native bathhouses. The fact was, the "whale" was a log raft—a veritable whale of a log raft.

This particular kind of log raft was a thousand feet long and it was being towed down the Columbia on a Pacific Ocean voyage to San Diego, California—eleven hundred miles south. It was one of the first of the many

Benson rafts which made West Coast logging history for thirty-five years.

Simon Benson was one of Portland, Oregon's great benefactors. From Viking ancestors, the Norway-born farmer settled first in Wisconsin and then came West in 1885 to work as blacksmith in John Beavis's logging camp near St. Helens, Oregon. He bought his own timber and five years later was logging with bulls near Portland.

With two men named Ordway and Weidler he acquired some secondhand rails, a few old trucks, and a rickety locomotive, and became the first railroad logger in the Pacific Northwest—in the timber near Cathlamet and the Indian country of Clatskanie. It was here his inventive brain conceived the idea of a log raft that would withstand the buffetings of the wild Pacific Ocean.

Simon Benson's plan was based on the failure of Captain Hugh Robertson to build successful seagoing rafts—big enough to be profitable and strong enough to make a voyage. Too many of Captain Robertson's rafts had been broken up by gales or their towing hawsers had snapped and the logs had drifted away into sea wastes. Benson had new ideas. One day in 1906, he slapped the broad back of Ole J. Evenson, his partner in the Benson Timber Company.

"All night I could not sleep. I hear the ocean pound bang-bang and chains creaking. There is no ocean here on the Columbia River, O. J., yet all night I hear it. You know what? It is the big raft we are going to build and send to sea."

"Simon!" Partner Evenson thundered. "There is no heat here either but you're crazy with it, just the same.

You can't build such a raft. Robertson was a good raft builder, and he lost millions of feet of prime fir logs. His rafts were too heavy to launch and tow. Now it is you!"

"Sure, sure," Simon Benson agreed, good-naturedly, "it is me—and I am not Captain Robertson. But you and I want to build a sawmill in San Diego and we want to get some good logs down there with lumber to build the mill. Now I know what to do. I roll around in my bunk and hear those waves splashing on the logs and I know how to build good, seaworthy rafts."

Evenson stood open-mouthed in wonder yet also open-eared as Simon Benson spun his fancy tale and described the method he had devised. To build the first raft meant risking all the assets of the firm and all the money it could borrow—in addition to a hundred thousand dollars in saw logs and sawed lumber. Evenson might have agreed with anybody who had called Simon Benson daft but he himself could not call him that. He knew too well his partner was a genius. He had the utmost respect for the rough-hewn logger and was willing to gamble his share of the business, to put himself forever in debt. Gamble? Simon Benson saw none in the venture. There was nothing ahead but success.

"You go right away," he told his younger partner, "and hire John Fastabend, the railroad builder. He is in Astoria and can build the cradle the way I want it. O. J.—the secret is in a floating cradle that will hold the logs until the raft is finished and then can be jerked loose away from it."

John A. Fastabend listened to Evenson's offer and decided to take the contract. He had come to Astoria from

Salt Lake City in 1892 to take charge of the building of a railroad between Astoria and Hillsboro. When plans for this fell through, he built breakwaters and jetties at Smith's Point.

"I think Simon Benson has had one dream too many," he said, "but I'll talk to him. He's a fine man—honest and capable. I'd be happy to work with him."

Benson's cradle was a reality within a month. It was built in Wallace Slough, a backwater in the Columbia River, and safe from salt-water toredos which would have eaten up the timbers within a year. To the curious settlers of the lower reaches of the river the cradle looked like the "bare bones of a ship." The bowl-shaped trusses, heavily reinforced, formed the bottom and sides, similar to a vessel's ribs. The structure was eight hundred feet long, forty feet wide in the middle and thirty feet from "keel" to top rails—built in sections fastened together by toggles in an interlocking device. One side of the cradle was moored to piles driven deep in the river bottom.

As John Fastabend bolted timber to timber, Simon Benson and his partner had crews cutting the trees that would take the long sea voyage. They chose the tall, straight firs, from fifty to one hundred feet long—pole trees rather than forest giants, for more ease in handling and fitting into the raft. The tops and all limbs were lopped off, bark pried away to save weight and space. Fir bark would absorb water where green wood repelled it. The logs were then hauled to the slough and held in booms.

The floating derrick used in building the cradle towed the log booms close to it. Simon Benson stood on its deck like some early Viking chief riding the prow of his long-ship. As the grab hook sank into a log, the steam donkey jerking and jumping, the lift boom strained under the weight of the swinging log and the derrick rocked like a barge in a storm.

"Pack them in just right," the big logger said. "That's what we have to do—end to end, then a log on top to hold the butted ends together."

Six men with pike poles, peavies, and axes rode the rising deck of the raft. When the hook dropped a log they wrestled it into place, turning it and chopping away any protruding knot or burl so it would fit tightly. It was a job of weaving the logs together for greatest strength. As the layers increased, so did the width as well as the weight, cradle and logs sinking gradually under the surface of the water. The outside logs at each end were brought to a point to form a wall within which the inner logs were laced together. Each end of the raft protruded a hundred feet beyond tne cradle form.

When the raft was about half completed, a two-and-a-half-inch stud anchor chain was laid through the center, paralleling the logs, from end to end. Over each pointed end of the raft was fitted a nose guard of boiler plate holding a heavy iron ring for securing the towing hawser. More chains were shackled to the spine chain and as more logs were stacked they were woven over and under, the ends dangling at the edge of the raft.

When the great cigar-shaped bulk was rounded almost to completion, several hundred thousand feet of sawed timbers and boards were worked in. For a top deck came cedar poles, spars, shingles, and lath—all to be used in the building of the San Diego sawmill. Around the entire girth more chains were looped and linked tight with the ends of those used inside the raft.

On the drizzly morning of June 26, 1906, forty-two days after the loading of the cradle had begun, Simon Benson proudly ordered the sections of it pulled apart. It was a dramatic occasion—a crowning moment in his active life. If the raft was not built and balanced perfectly, it would list to port or starboard like a ship with a hole in her side, and be unfit for deep-sea towing. Anxiously the builder watched the men removing the toggle bars and pulling away each section of the cradle. Partner Evenson stood beside him, waiting stolidly. Everything the two owned was tied up in this experiment. The final unit of the cradle was pulled back—and the men saw their masterpiece floating evenly and serenely.

Simon Benson stood entranced. He saw success in the great bulk—one thousand feet long, fifty-five feet across, with a depth of thirty-five feet, more than half of which was under water. He jerked his head and pounded his fists.

"She's right. O. J.—we've done a good job—Mr. Fastabend, you, all of our men. She's just like I've seen her all along."

His partner sighed with amazement and felt equally satisfied. But he was the cautious one—the firm's safety valve. "You think she'll take all the pounding the sea will give her? A lot of weight there. Simon—you know how much chain we've got in that raft? I know. I had it made—and you won't believe it. Almost two hundred tons!"

"Not a pound too much," Benson replied. "That chain

has to hold together four and a half million feet of logs—
close to a hundred thousand dollars' worth. Now—is she
going to ride the sea all right? I'm saying she will—but
we may have done some things wrong. A man on the
towing tug could watch her actions and see how she
behaves. Know who that man is going to be? Well, it's
you."

Two stern-wheel river tugs churned into the slough
and with hawsers looped through the ring in the raft's
nose plate, the strange cargo moved with majesty and
poise out into the Columbia's mainstream and down
across the treacherous, shifting shoal waters of its mouth.
Off Peacock Spit a heavy-duty sea tug took over, paying
out six hundred feet of line and settling down in the
swells to the full power thrust of her steam-driven
pistons.

With binoculars trained on the heaving raft, Evenson
stood on the tug's after grating. For three days the tow
moved steadily into the gathering force of a southwest
gale, keeping a few miles offshore, the raft putting no
undue stress on the eight-inch manila hawser. The waves
continued to build up, most of them washing over the
logs, the bigger ones breaking halfway along the raft's
length. The watcher could then detect the elastic give of
the whole structure.

Then the wind veered into the west and the tug was
forced to alter her course to starboard, taking the gale on
her quarter. This was the real test for the raft. The waves
now battered it from the side and if it was not seaworthy
the heaving walls of water would rock it so violently or
slew it from side to side with such force, the hawser would

snap or the steady drag would be so great the tug could not keep it in the seaway.

For four days the gale kept up its blasting and then eased into squalls and clearing weather. Relaxing his vigil, O. J. Evenson went below to have a mug of coffee with the mate of the tug.

"We'll make it now if your engines hold out."

The mate nodded. "I couldn't ask for a better tow. She rides steadier than a barge full of sea gulls."

Seven days later they entered the harbor of San Diego —the first Benson raft a success. A telegram reached its builder two weeks after it had left the Columbia River.

> RAFT HERE SAFELY NOW BEING BROKEN DOWN
> MAKE SECOND ONE JUST SAME   OJE

One hundred and twenty Benson rafts followed this first one on the eleven-hundred-mile sea journey, from 1906 to 1941—almost ten million dollars in logs transported to the Benson Timber Company mill in San Diego. Many carried deck loads of machinery battened tight with sailcloth. Only four rafts were lost or broken up and many of these logs were found and salvaged.

The rafts made Simon Benson rich and famous. He had succeeded where others had failed and no one ever tried to build seagoing rafts in competition. The San Diego sawmill continued to thrive with the steady source of Douglas fir from Oregon. Long after Simon Benson's death he was known as the man who sent the forests out to sea—the rafts that looked like whales.

XV

California . . . 1906

SPRING DRIVE ON THE PIT

"Now then, feller," a grizzled hillbilly on a mule once told Whitewater Jim Carney, "onless a man's got bear blood and wildcat's feet on him, he ain't got license to go ridin' logs down that Pit River. Dassent lay down and take a drink outen her. So doggone swift she'll tear a man's teeth right outen his face. You figurin' to drive logs on the Pit?"

"Yes, I am," Jim Carney told him, "and I can't wait to get there. Old man—you've got to have wild water to drive logs on and the Pit's the pick of 'em all—including the Payette up in Idaho and the Kettle in B.C. Can't wait to get into my three-lakes shoes."

That was the way river driver Jim Carney felt about the Pit River. It was shorter than some of the other wild ones but it made up for that in a hurry—roaring down out of the pine country to flow into the easygoing Sacramento. And Jim couldn't wait to get there, to get the feel of the bucking, rolling logs under his sharp-shod steel calks, to make high jinks with the Indian squaws and fighting breed of men that lived for the hell-for-leather profession of driving logs on white water.

You had to belong to this breed to survive. You had to look at the river plunging down out of the canyon—curling, frothing, biting at the rocks, leveling out placidly then falling into more swirls, falls, and rapids—look at it and grin clear down to your knobby knees. You had to be half cougar and an acrobatic one at that. You had to climb a log jam with a peavy and help twenty other river pigs wrestle the logs out of the tangle. With the water boiling all around a center jam, you had to row a *bateau*, poke, pry, and dynamite the sticks back into motion. You had to fight your way to glory with hands, feet, and teeth and dance to an Indian fiddle when the work was done. This was what you did to earn your three dollars a day.

Jim Carney—Whitewater Jim—was one of these rough, tough, stouthearted rivermen—French, Irish, and bobcat out of the Michigan woods. "The devil's own spawn," he said of himself, but he would stop to listen to a bird singing and pick a wildflower for an Indian child. The river was his life and he made the most of it.

In May, 1906, he landed in Redding with Dapper Dan Mahoney, known as the Bear, with whom he had logged on the Manistee in Michigan, many years before. They had been driving logs on the Grand Ronde in Oregon when Charlie McSherry, the *bateau* builder, told them the drive was about ready on the Pit. Now they rolled into Pat Murphy's House of Hospitality on California Street.

"Yer as welcome as a pair o' sweet colleens, you two dirty-lookin' bums. What're ye havin'? Gin Pole John is expectin' you lads. He's been askin'."

And Gin Pole John, river boss of the Redding and Big Bend Lumber Company, was not far away. He greeted Jim Carney with the playful enthusiasm of a Saint Bernard. "Where are the rest of the boys?"

"They're due—stompin' their feet and ready to go. When is that, John?"

"You can go to camp as soon as you help us put the boom in at the mill here at Redding. You can work in the woods for ten days if you're a mind to. Or you can dangle around here for that time. I'll square you for room and board at the Temple. How about it?"

"I'll take the Temple, John," said Carney. "I'll send my outfit up and Mahoney and myself will go by heel and toe. What you say, Dan?"

"I'm hankerin' for to stay." A wounded deer look came into the Bear's eye. His six feet of brawn sagged. "I took me a walk to look at the bootiful snow-peaked mountings and what did I see? As purty a brown-eyed quarter breed as ever there was this side of the Highwayen Islands. Sure it's the country I'll settle down in."

"Settle down!" Jim Carney hooted. "Why, you moony-lookin' freak—you wouldn't settle down as long as there's free fare to purgatory. Listen to him, Gin Pole. I'll speak for the two of us. We'll help you swing the boom and then high-tail for camp. Come on, you shanty Irisher. We'll get us a feed of chilikillarney."

"Wait a minute, boys," Gin Pole John called after them. "I got something to pass over to you. Your friend Charlie McSherry was here and I sent him ahead to build some boats. But he had to take a shanty on one eye with him. There is a tough bartender two doors up at Farrell's

Saloon. Whatever his name is, it's bogus and so is everything he talks about. He claims he trained to fight John L. Sullivan but got hit on the head and couldn't go through with it. Well, he told McSherry this and the lad called him an empty windbag. Bogus then leans over the bar and hands McSherry the shanty. Your friend promised Bogus two for one as soon as you two arrived. Bogus said 'Bring the river rats in here and I'll hand 'em each a bigger shiner than you've got.' So there you have it, boys."

The tale was one Dan Mahoney relished and what he intended doing about it he relished even more. He pounded the bar, sidestepped out the swinging doors, and with Jim Carney behind him, strode into Farrell's saloon. The bartender, now known as Bogus, was standing behind the bar bulldog fashion, jaw jutting out, hands on hips. When Dapper Dan stepped to the bar, he growled:

"What will yuhs have?"

Mahoney had the answer ready. "A shanty like you passed to McSherry. You got another?"

"That I have," said the bartender, starting the punch.

Mahoney grabbed the fist. "Oh, is that it?" he asked and almost jerked the arm out of Bogus' shoulder. Then he placed his boot against the bar and Bogus was on his way over it, his belt buckle scraping mahogany. In a minute he was on his back from two of Mahoney's bone-crushing blows. A third and fourth broke his nose and blood was running from it.

"Is he hand-painted enough?" Dapper Dan asked Jim Carney. They decided he was and Charlie McSherry's black eye was avenged.

The next morning they went to Turtle Bay and helped swing the log boom across the main channel of the river and anchor it to the opposite side. The channel was now ready to corral the logs for the sawmill.

They could have ridden the stage to camp but the fare was five dollars apiece. Instead they left their outfits to be picked up by one of the company's ten-horse teams now coming down from the woods. It was important these arrived on time and in good condition. They couldn't go down with the drive without the proper gear—especially the black boomer Stetson hat, full crown, with three-inch brim that turned up fore and aft like the ends of a river *bateau*. And they need the tailored coats, top shirts, stagged pants, and three-lakes boots with steel calks.

"I feel like walkin'," said Dapper Dan. "It's better than bein' under the sheriff's clock. We'll start out tonight with the moon smilin' down on us and the owls seein' us safely down the path."

Two mornings later they reached the mountain village of Montgomery Creek and joined two other river men— Big Archie and Brigham who had just come in on the stage. The four took a trail through the woods and struck the logging camp on a creek a few miles in. The first sounds they heard were lusty shouts and then from the river driver's camp across the stream came a throaty crooning:

> Oh, my name is Sam'l Hall, Sam'l Hall.
> Yes, my name is Sam'l Hall, Sam'l Hall.
> Oh, my name is Sam'l Hall—
> You're a gang o' muckers all

And I hate you one and all—
By my soul!

Oh, I killed a man they said, so they said.
Yes, I killed a man they said, so they said.
Oh, I killed a man they said
For I hit him on the head
And I left him there for dead,
By my soul!

So up the rope I'll go, I will go.
Yes, up the rope I'll go, I will go.
Oh, up the rope I'll go
With the crowd all down below
Yelling, "Sam—I told you so!"
By my soul!

The voice died in a welling burst of guffaws as the singer was seized bodily and tossed into the creek water. He crawled up the muddy bank, sputtering and cursing, and attempted to break up a ring of men playing cards on a stump. Then the four newcomers were greeted with more shouts, stag-shirted men calling from horse barn, bunkhouses, blacksmith shop, and wagon shed.

"All ready for the run, Jim Carney? Good old White-water Jim and Dapper Dan Mahoney. Three million feet of sugar and white pine layin' out in the river waitin' for you. Boys—meet Ike Tremont. Best old horned toad I ever logged with. There goes the dinner bell. Come one, come all!"

The cookee was sounding the gong, camp help and river men crowding around the door. Mountains of food came in on steaming platters as cups and plates were hammered on the plank tables. Coffee and tea flowed freely as did yarns around the barrel stove and campfire afterward.

"Yessir, we would take a heavy oak keg and drive spikes inward near the bottom and put honey inside. The bear would poke his head into the honey and when he tried to pull it out, the nails stuck in his neck. We usually got there in time."

"Down to Shovel Pass we had a barrel trick too. We would knock the end out of one and put a burlap sack over it, running a heavy rope through the sack. A new man would be told there was a bobcat in there and they would bet five dollars he couldn't pull him out. If he bit, the newcomer would take hold of the rope, brace himself for a big pull and when the rope came out with nothing on it, the fellow would go flying on his heels. It was a real sucker game because sometimes they did put a bobcat or bear in the barrel and would bet money no dog could get him out. No dog ever could."

Gin Pole John was everywhere, counting the men, making up crews, checking on boats, tools, and equipment. "We start for the river at six," he ordered. "And all you buzzards that go to the buck-and-wing at the hot springs tonight, stay away from them Indian gals. Modoc braves've got sharp knives. And I need you all on the river at sunup."

Then the drive started. Logs clogged the river, which was narrow and quiet at this high elevation. Blankets, grub, and oars were piled into the three flat-bottomed *bateaux,* other men crow-hopping out over the floating floor of yellow and brown logs with peavies and cant hooks ready. A few dragged sleepily behind, the river boss urging them to action.

The boom sticks holding the logs together were pulled apart and the front sticks set adrift. As they moved out the drivers on them leaped back on the logs behind. When a third of the whole mass had been loosened, the boom sticks were toggled together again. Now the freed logs were floating faster, being sucked into the millstream. One by one the men jumped for the boats. The Pit River drive was on.

At first the boats stayed well behind. The channel was narrow, hemmed in by rocky flanges, the logs crowding them, choking the defile, river water cascading down over them. Pressure on the forward logs sent them spinning, rolling, and tumbling on down, the others following like sheep after a leader.

Now the river opened up and the mass spread out, divided, the section toward the south bank slipping on down in the fast current, the larger bunch hanging up in the backwater. The boats came in and Jim Carney was one of the first out. He jumped three logs at a time to reach the forward end on the stalled parade. Two other drivers joined him and they guided the lazy pine out, log by log, until the current sent them spinning. Then the following ones flowed steadily into the suction of the mainstream.

Another mile and the logs had fallen into an orderly procession, eight and ten abreast. Swiftly they passed around a big bend and then were skating and skittering over rapids. Now came one of the bad spots—the first real white water.

A series of barriers appeared in the river, the water piling up in a roaring fury, boiling over the tops of the rocks, spewing froth and foam as it swept on down across a bouldered bar.

The first logs struck the rocks and a few went end-over-end. Others came smashing in by the hundreds, the fore-runners trapped in their attempts to clear the rocks. In a thundering few minutes the jam was tight, the great pile growing higher as every wild lunge of the river tossed up more logs and boiled against the obstruction it had made. Unable to surmount the dam, the water curled around it, slashing halfway up the canyon side.

The three *bateaux* came swooping up in the current and wedged themselves into the jumble. Men swarmed over the mountain, none shouting now as nothing could be heard above the tumult of wild water, the sounds magnified in volume as they bounced back and forth between the rock walls.

At the face of the jam, bound fast to the solid barrier, a dozen men pried with peavies, trying to loosen the top logs to get at the lower ones—pressing, twisting, rolling them as best they could. But the nest, the key to the tangle, was still buried, and the work became doubly dangerous. As they wrestled more logs free any of the ones below might spring up suddenly, the whole mass smothering and crushing the drivers or flinging them off like loose bark. Instead the jam now came apart with a flattening crash and every man jumped clear. The two who slipped into the river were boat-hooked to safety.

Once more the drive was pitching headlong down the swift watercourse. Three miles on the logs slid and slithered like dead fish over a twenty-foot fall. The *bateaux* made shore and the drivers paid out line to ease them over the drop, catfooting themselves across the ledge rocks as the boats jerked on ahead. Once more afloat, the three craft bobbed and spun, held on course by the rudder men. Downstream a wing jam appeared but it was quickly broken up. The logs swam more easily in ten miles of quiet water and then in the gathering dusk piled up in another twisted tangle.

Gin Pole John maneuvered his boat ashore and swung his arm for the others to follow. The men made a rough camp and cooks roasted bear meat in tin ovens over the open fire. Blankets were unrolled and the drivers slept like tired sheep dogs. At daybreak the river boss was shouting and prodding them awake, his plan of breaking the jam already made. The logs were heaped up on a gravel spit around which the river made a bend.

"We'll blow out the bend—bust up the sand instead of the logs—and let the river push them through. They're spread out so wide it'd take a half dozen heavy charges to do any good and that'd wreck a passel of good pine."

The first blast sent boulders and spray flying high, splintering only the logs directly over the dynamite. The second explosion opened the channel wide and the river roared through the new course, carrying a mad rush of logs with it. The lagging ones were rounded and sent into the millstream. The drive was underway again.

And it was ended almost as suddenly. After a third day of herding the logs over shallows and rock-studded white water, Jim Carney saw the stack of the sawmill at Turtle Bay. The front-running logs had already struck the angled swing boom and were drifting in to the mill crews. He jumped on a big ponderosa and stopped its roll with calks and peavy. One of the boats caught up to the log and he saw Dapper Dan Mahoney flat in the bottom of it.

"Get out of there, you lazy goat!" he shouted with feigned disgust. "We ain't got the drive in yet."

Mahoney grinned through his pain. "I got three ribs you could hang your Stetson on. Log tried to fight me. You got to finish the drive for both of us, Whitewater."

Carney did. The wagon teams took the crew back for the second push and then the third. At the end of it came the big celebration in Redding when Whitewater Jim, with river and woods crews, "blew her in." He went north to the Oregon and Idaho rivers but never forgot the Pit, and always came back to it when the drive was on. Jim Carney finished many a drive for men who would not be pushing logs when the last one was button-hooked at the swing boom.

XVI

Washington . . . 1909

THEY HARNESSED THE WILD LOGS

RAIN was one thing the pioneer inhabitants of Washington's West Coast were sure they would get. Potatoes might be scarce and Christmas presents scanty but of rain they were sure to have plenty—in all forms from nagging drizzles to wild squalls off the Pacific Ocean. What else but rain caused the trees to grow in such profusion and to such great size?

For back of Grays Harbor lay the greatest forest of big timber on the face of the earth. It ran north for eighty miles to Cape Flattery and the Strait of Juan de Fuca, south to the Columbia River and east to the Cascade Mountains. All this great wealth of timber—Douglas fir, Western red cedar, and hemlock—was kept green and growing by almost continual rain six months of the year and occasional showers and storms the other six months.

In November, 1909, however, this loggers' friend and patron saint had become a menace almost as bad as the forest fires it drenched. For five weeks water had been falling in the Grays Harbor country, not with a friendly patter but with a vicious downpour. Torrents and cloudbursts had raged over the countryside, swelling the Satsop and Chehalis rivers to dangerous degrees. Still the rain came bucketing down and the rivers rose until they burst over their banks into the scattered farm and stump lands.

In the lower reaches of the Chehalis this November lay 20,000,000 feet of logs, some 50,000 in what was called the Chehalis Boom. Several loggers had been running logs into the corrals, intending to sort them out later, and tow them to sawmills in Aberdeen, Hoquiam, and Cosmopolis. But the river defeated their purpose. The rain kept pouring down and one dismal dawn saw the big Chehalis Boom broken wide and the logs gone wild, charging for the open sea, twenty-two miles away.

The logging firm of Schafer Brothers owned more than half of the logs which they had worked all summer to cut and which represented many thousands of dollars, almost all their assets. The three Schafer brothers—Albert, Hubert, and Peter—were young, enterprising, and daring. They saw the disaster and knew only one answer. They had to get those logs back or "go broke." Other loggers saw the timber floating out to tidewater and shook their heads in sorrow. The three Schafer brothers were too busy to shake their heads. The story of their rescue of the stampeding logs is a Grays Harbor epic.

Peter was 24, Hubert 20, and Albert 14 when they persuaded their parents to let them log some prime trees on the home place, a farm on the Satsop River.

"All right, boys," agreed John D. and Anna Schafer, "on the condition that you hire Ben Kesterson as boss and take orders from him, and that you get all your farm work done."

So under the hand of Ben Kesterson, who was an experienced logger, a skid road was built over which logs would be hauled to the river. A small crew was hired, two of whom were Indians—Billy Quaick, as log bucker who cut the fallen trees into workable lengths, and Hyasman, as general handyman, faller, canoe builder, and bull cook. Oxen were purchased and soon the Schafer woods echoed to the stirring call "Timmmberrr!" as giant firs came crashing down to earth. And down the skid road came the long string of bulls—five yoke of them, red, white, and spotted animals, lurching to and fro and up and down, wheezing, grunting, coughing, with young Pete walking near the lead pair, waving his goad stick, praising and blasting the powerful beasts.

Behind the bulls came the big logs—six and eight feet in diameter, forty feet along—bumping and rolling over the skids, which were short logs half buried in the dirt. Behind the hooves of the last two bulls, just ahead of the lead log, the skid greaser darted in and out, while riding the last log majestically was Albert, youngest member of the Schafer clan, ready to unhook the logs when they reached the landing by the river.

This action was accompanied by a booming range of sounds—the grunts of the oxen and the thud of their heavy hoofs, Peter Schafer's yells as he jabbed the steel spur of the goad stick in the flanks of bulls that were not pulling, the earth-bound rumble of the logs on the skids. Perhaps Albert was walking beside the logs now and perhaps the "turn" had plowed into a bank of dirt and snagged to a stop. It was then his job, with the help of Ben Kesterson's son Ed, to move by means of a "sampson" the log that was stuck. The sampson was simply a sturdy pole, one end jammed into the ground, the other in the crotch dogs of the lead log. The boys put their weight on the free end of the pole and when the oxen pulled again, the log would roll away from the obstruction.

The Schafer day was a long one. At four o'clock in summer and five in winter, the boys crawled out of their bunks to feed and card the bulls, clean the stables, feed and milk the thirty-odd dairy cows, and then have breakfast. After logging was done in the evening there were more farm chores, fences to mend, and bears to chase out of the orchard. In winter and summer they shot deer, elk, and bear, and speared salmon for the camp table. With the help of the Indians they fashioned dugout canoes, thirty-two feet long, out of cedar logs and with peavies and pike poles aided the log drives down the Satsop. The logs were sold to the A. J. West sawmill and others in "the Harbor"—two million feet of them in 1897.

This was the year Hubert Schafer joined the rush to the Klondike to pick the gold which was said to line the banks of the Yukon River. He escaped the great avalanche at Sheep Camp, aided in the rescue of many bodies, and returned to Grays Harbor much wiser if no richer. And then another event occured—a real tragedy. Father John D. Schafer died. The young brothers were on their own.

"We need a donkey," Peter said one day. "Bull teams are too slow. They're using steam engines and cables to pull the logs, from here to Eureka, California, where that fellow Dolbeer invented the upright spool donkey. How about it?"

"You're right," Hubert agreed. "I'll go to Seattle and see about it."

He went to Seattle and to work in an iron foundry which manufactured the new donkey engine and in a year had learned the technicalities of its operation from boiler tubes to valve fittings. At home Peter and Albert fattened the bulls for the beef market, set aside butter-and-cream money and made the first payment on a 9 x 10 road engine complete with a drum of steel cable. The "little wonder" was floated down the Satsop on a barge, set up in the Schafer yard while Hubert explained the workings of the gauges, levers, and gears. Even Hyasman, the Indian laborer, grunted his approval. He could see his work getting easier.

"He no eat hay. Good. He no need stable. Good."

The boys could hardly wait to get the engine started. Hubert directed the crew in cutting billets of wood and stoking the fire while others took their broadaxes and hewed two fir trees into giant sled runners. Peter took a few turns of the cable around a stump and, snorting, groaning, stuttering, and bouncing, the donkey pulled itself up on the sled and was bolted fast.

Dinner was also bolted that noon and the men hurried back to the newfangled contraption that was destined to replace the bulls. An hour later the donkey had jerked itself to a location about a quarter of a mile from camp and was ready to go to work. A horse, whose name should have gone down in history but was never recorded, hauled the end of the cable from the donkey to where the trees had been felled. A short length of cable was looped around the first log and fastened to the main line, and Albert Schafer yelled:

"Let her go!"

Hubert was tending the throttle and he let steam into the cylinder. The drum turned, line whipped up from the ground and went taut. Then steam whistled through the valves, the donkey jumped and bounced. The log jerked forward, rolled, and spun, but kept moving. Hubert shot another jet of steam and the log came to a grinding stop a few feet from the sled—a perfect landing for the first steam-yarded log on the Satsop River.

The three enterprising Schafer brothers were now steam loggers and the donkey was whisking logs out of the brush faster than bulls with wings. It also helped open up log jams on the rivers and rescue stray logs which had left the swollen stream to wander into farmers' fields. It saved many lawsuits by doing so.

Some of the ranchers downriver resented the Schafers' violation of the woods and the success they were making. One day Albert reported: "You know that fellow Snead down below? You know he's got forty or more prime fir logs setting there on his place with a 'For Sale' sign on them? He never logged a day in his life. He hasn't got a bull and one of his horses couldn't pull a beehive over. Know whose logs they are? Ours. He's stolen them out of the river."

And so the poleax brand, identifying Schafer Brothers logs, was originated. Before a log was rolled into the river, the steel forging in the shape of a poleax, was driven against each end. This did not stop all the pirating as some poachers would simply saw off the ends of the logs, leaving no proof that the logs were Schafer's. But whenever suspicion was pointed in some rancher's direction, one of the crew would be dispatched to keep a close watch and catch the poacher in the act of sawing off the branded ends. There were then legal and other means of stopping the practice.

And then came 1909—and the raging flood which broke up the Chehalis Boom and sent fifty thousand logs cruising out to sea to be lost in the swells and breakers. The Schafer brothers, always alert, always the forerunners when chances had to be taken, jumped into action. Rushing young Ed Kesterson ahead of him into one of the dugout canoes, Hubert shouted:

"I'll slip down to the Island by Cosmopolis and round up any logs I can there. Six of our men are following Ed and me. You fellows get down to Aberdeen in a hurry and see if all the tugs are out. Get on one and see that it's our logs they get!"

There were eight small tugboats in operation on Grays Harbor and only one in sight when Albert and Peter arrived at the flooded town. The raging river covered all the docks and now reached into the streets, lifting the plank sidewalks and carrying them away with sheds and frame buildings. Floating past the tug *Edgar* were chicken coops, outhouses, pieces of barns, and the bloated carcass of a cow. The *Edgar* was tied to some piling near a sawmill, with Captain Tom Soule smoking his pipe and shaking his head at the debris and desolation.

"Hey, Tom!" Albert shouted as their canoe pulled up. "What's the matter? She broke down? All the other boats are out . . ."

A drawn and haggard stare from Captain Soule stifled further words. Albert could clearly see something was wrong and knew the skipper would explain it when he wanted to.

"Son—everybody's out and goin' crazy." The master waved his arm toward the open sea. "We been out in that whirlygig of logs since the boom busted. It's worth your life to mix up with them trees goin' every which way, includin' sideways and end for end. My men quit. They're plain tuckered out and starved—and me too!"

Peter clutched at the tug's rail. "How about us—Albert and me—Captain Tom? Will you take her out again with us as the crew? There's a lot of Schafer logs that have got to be brought home. How about it, skipper? We're good hands—Albert and me."

"Get aboard!" the captain boomed. "I don't know a Schafer log from a wildcat but I know a couple of Schafer working stiffs. Throw off that hitch. Who's runnin' the engine?"

Both boys jumped for the deck and Albert scuttled down the ladder to the engine room. He knew very little about marine engines but the situation was desperate. He quickly sized up the forward and reverse levers, the steam attachments and gauges. Almost at once came the jangling bell signal which showed "Ahead" on the dial. He let steam in and the tug all but leaped out of the water.

Peter stood in the bow and shouted directions to Captain Soule at the wheel. The tug sped out into the bounding, rearing, raging welter of logs, planks, and assorted flotsam. Peter had a hawk's eye for logs with the poleax brand and when he had one pulled close with his cant hook, he slipped a line around it and took it in tow. When seven or eight logs were trailing, the tug ran them back into the river where a temporary corral was made—and then out again on another foray.

Thousands of logs had already been caught in the twisting tides and currents and swept out over the Grays Harbor bar, but many other thousands were still bobbing in the foam and swells. With hardly a minute's rest the crew of three kept on rounding up Schafer logs, filling the first corral and fencing off another. The only breaks in the frantic push were to load firewood and take on some of the regular crew, now rested and willing to work again. After ten hours the men stopped to eat and then the race began again.

This time, with seven men aboard, the *Edgar* drove out into the rougher water of the outer harbor, even across the bar into the heaving seas. For two days, they moved in and out, saving the logs which lesser men would have given up as hopelessly lost. Even in the black of night they kept going, identifying the poleax imprint on the log ends by feeble light and almost superhuman insight.

"But that Pete," Captain Soule said later. "He didn't need no light to see by. Part owl, that one is. He could see that Schafer brand if it was hid under the bark."

Fifty thousand logs broke loose in the Chehalis Boom—more than half of them belonging to the Schafer Brothers. Many million feet of timber was lost to the tides and for years afterward logs from the disaster kept drifting in to the beaches of Washington and Oregon, perhaps even Japan and China. But the Schafer boys saved all that human energy and initiative could and it kept them solvent. Captain Tom Soule had nothing but praise for their work on those three memorable days.

"Albert was a little bit shaky on them engine levers at first. He wasn't so good at stopping but he was one of the greatest go-aheaders I ever saw. And he was pretty powerful at backing up. I'd give him a bell to go ahead. That tug would almost leap out of the water, like a black fish. When I wanted reverse, she'd back with a bang that would make your jaw rattle. Finally, when we were all done with that log catching, I told Albert to stop the engine. 'How do you do that, captain?' he yelled at me. 'Haven't caught on to that yet.' But sufferin' snakes, he could sure make her go forward and back!"

XVII

Washington . . . 1912

RED SKY OVER HUNTING CREEK

FOR twenty days it had been forest-fire weather—hot and dry. The whole west slope of Beard Mountain was considered in extreme danger. Smoke was reported every day and small blazes sprang up in some parched areas. No fire within a hundred miles had got beyond the brush stage so far, but most of the logging companies were operating with reasonable care.

The woods around Hunting Creek had been considered comparatively safe since the area was higher in the mountains, the fog raising the humidity, and it had never suffered a serious fire. In spite of this Superintendent Homer McGee had closed down two camps and posted fire spotters at the other two—Headquarters Camp 2 and Camp 4 six miles up the creek. They were "highball" operations, using steam donkey engines and high lead cables between spar trees—all of which meant, "Get more logs out quicker."

This company policy had been laid down in spite of many earlier fires in Washington and Oregon, caused by speed-at-all-costs methods. One fire had sprung up near Enumclaw and had all but wiped out the mill and town.

The area around Chehalis and Olympia had also suffered great damage in other fires and two logging camps near Hoquiam had been destroyed with valuable timber. Sixty families were homeless in a section along the Sol Duc River.

Homer McGee had personal reasons for being as cautious as his job would allow. Two brothers and all he had himself owned had been lost in the Lewis and Clark Counties fires ten years before. That had not been a single fire but a vicious series of them and the flames had sprung up so quickly twenty-five people had been caught as they were fleeing from their homes. A dozen villages and settlements, another dozen sawmills and shingle mills, hundreds of farm and stump ranches had been wiped out in the holocaust that spread smoke, cinders, and gloom from Olympia, Washington to Eugene, Oregon. Almost a million acres of prime fir, spruce, and cedar had been destroyed in this Dark Day that lasted a week.

Logger McGee had a stout heart but he knew what terror a forest fire could strike in it, what abject desolation was left after the cyclone rush of timber burning. His memory of that fateful morning was very poignant. He was driving a team of horses hauling firewood for the cookhouse when the men in camp smelled smoke. They knew fires were burning somewhere but they did not know how close. Homer McGee dumped his load and started the team back up the rutty woods road. Two miles above camp the smoke was thicker and the air felt hotter than usual. He knew now the fire was not far off but he was young and foolhardy, not easily frightened.

Then suddenly it happened—and very swiftly. The road

wound along the bottom of a narrow ravine and in a few seconds a sheet of flame was roaring down upon him. Even the river seemed afire. Instinctively he tried to get the team turned around but he had no time to do more than jerk the lines.

Like a hurricane the V-shaped walls of fire roared down on him, exploding as flames raced along. The boy jumped and dove headlong into the river already hot to the touch. He buried himself as deeply as he could in the water and under the muddy overhang of roots. He prayed, living a horrible, scorching lifetime in the minutes it took the vanguard of the blast to pass over him.

The aftermath was something he always tried to forget but never could. When he dared crawl out over the hot ashes and still glowing cover, he saw the charred horses on the ground and four big iron hoops—all that remained of the wagon. He crawled along the edge of the river and finally picked his way through the smoking snags to the log landing, marked by the twisted pile of rusted steel that had been the donkey engine. Some of the men had escaped, he learned. Eight others, including his two brothers, had perished in the inferno.

Now, ten years later, the memory was still so sharp, Superintendent McGee would have shut down all operations if he had had the authority to do so. But the log-hungry bosses were shouting for more timber all the time and he had to keep the crews going. And so, on the morning of August 4, 1912, Homer McGee kept an eagle's watch on headquarters and warned the men firing the donkey at Camp 4 to be doubly careful and keep several water barrels handy.

There was no spark-arrester screen over the yarding engine's stack. When the fire door was opened to rake the fire and stoke it with another dozen slabs of wood and bark, the draft sent billows of smoke and hot sparks shooting into the air. Yet the donkey was set well out from the fringe of timber close to the log landing and the sparks were generally cooled by the time any fell into the dry evergreen needles and brush.

By eleven o'clock the morning fog had been evaporated by the sun and a fresh westerly wind, which added to the heat and discomfort of the men as they kept up their fast pace. Out in the woods a choker was set around a big fir section, the rigging slinger waved his arm with a "Yip!" and the whistle punk gave a jerk of the cord which sounded the donkey's shrill "Peep!"

Up out of the tangle of logs and slash came the log, threshing and slapping like something alive as it dangled from the block. The main line of steel came tight, then slacked, and as the donkey puncher shot in the steam, the log went leaping and bucking toward the landing. It fell and leaped again, swinging out across the cluttered cover.

By all the rules the log should have stopped at the "hot deck" when it came bouncing into the landing. It did not. For some unaccountable reason the donkey puncher tightened the haulback line which lifted the log high without stopping. When he saw the big stick bearing down on him he shouted and jumped, the drums still winding line. The heavy log went on up, striking the block and then swung in a wide arc, smashing into the donkey engine.

Again the rules were violated. Bolted tightly to its skids the donkey took the crash solidly. But the impact broke the steam line and battered in the stack. There was a sudden puff of smoke out of the fire door and then a small hissing explosion of steam. In seconds a dozen small fires had sprung up in the flanking debris and brush.

Fireman, donkeyman, and wood buck jumped for the water buckets. Most of the small blazes were snuffed out almost before they were started. But the lively west wind fanned one or two and before the men could notice them, flames were running along the ground as though shot from a nozzle. And the forest was suddenly on fire. What Superintendent McGee had feared had happened.

In his geared Climax locomotive Engineer Buck Wilson had earlier that morning backed a string of empty log cars into the landing. He was leaning idly out of the cab window when the accident happened and he saw the line of cars paralleling the flaming fringe of timber. Figuring that the wind would sweep the fire into the train, he immediately jerked it ahead and ripped off four sharp blasts of the whistle.

The woods crew had seen the smoke and were already running in to the landing. But the fire ran faster. The men reached the log deck and started to climb on the engine as Engineer Wilson jumped down to uncouple it from the lead car. Before he could return to the controls, a sheet of searing heat and licking flames rolled over the Climax. All the men fled like rats from a sinking ship.

There was one hope left and the crew dashed for it—the hand-operated speeder. It sat on a short spur track downgrade from the landing and the men swarmed on to it, pumping for their lives down the track.

In Headquarters Camp, McGee heard the commotion as

he stood in the lean-to blacksmith shop. The drawn faces
of the men told him all he wanted to know. They came
running, shouting: "She's all on fire up above!"

As the full story tumbled out, the woods boss knew he
had to shut down at once. He ran to the "gut hammer"
by the cookhouse door—used to call the crew to meals—
and set the iron triangle ringing with blows of the track
spike. The donkey puncher picked up the signal and held
the whistle cord down in a series of staccato blasts. But
then Homer McGee hesitated. Should he get everybody
out to safety or send fire-fighting crews up the railroad and
Hunting Creek canyon to try to control the fire and keep
it from coming down?

From what he could judge of the fire from the jumbled
accounts of the Camp 4 men, he knew the latter course was
a forlorn hope. For once he forgot the dollar appetite of
the general office and thought of his men. They might
save some timber by losing hands, feet, and lives. Better
that they all got out whole.

Accordingly he barked orders to abandon camp, ordered
steam up in the second Climax, and prayed for rain or a
shift in the wind. Most of the men jumped into action,
only too ready to leave the area. But then the woods boss
saw his rigging slinger Carlie Reader with a .30-.30 rifle
in his hand and realized he had this maverick to handle.
Carlie Reader could always be counted on to disagree with
anybody, especially the majority. He was afraid of nothing
on earth, would walk into trouble with arms held wide,
yet never seemed to have as much of it as timid men did.

"Pack your turkey," McGee told him, "and get ready
to move. What've you got that gun for?"

"It's Joe Hart's," the steel rigger answered slowly. "I borrowed it. If there's a fire I'm going to get me a buck. There's always deer running ahead of a fire. Or maybe a bear. Besides I figure they hadn't ought to gone off and left that engine up to Camp 4."

The woods boss swore in disgust. "You crazy fool! Have you ever been in a forest fire before?"

"Well sure, Mr. McGee. I been a logger long enough for that. Look—I and three more are going to take that speeder back up there. Maybe the fire ain't as bad as the boys say it is. Maybe we can save that engine and I'll get me a buck . . ."

The superintendent gave him the back of his hand and spun away, now astonished to see several men paying no attention to him or his orders. Many others were hesitating, not packing their bedrolls or suitcases. And then the fighting heart won over the fearing mind. McGee realized he had not been thinking of the safety of his men as much as of his own. The men were not thinking of either. They wanted to save their jobs. And, Homer McGee said to himself, so do I.

"Hey you—everybody!" he shouted. "We're going up. Get axes, hazel hoes, saws, mattocks, and shovels. We'll take the lokey up and fight that fire if we can!"

Carlie Reader and the three volunteers had already pumped their way out of sight. The speeder had covered over a mile of the light grade before the smoke reached them. They were two miles up before they heard the sound of the fury. As he moved his shoulders down and up with the pump handle, Carlie kept his eye out for deer.

The hot breath of the fire crackling somewhere ahead

descended upon the strong backs of the four men. No animals appeared but dense smoke and ashy soot did, the air as dark as at dusk. Once they stopped for breath and two of the men slid down the ravine to cool their faces in the creek. When they returned their red eyes were set with determination.

"We're going back down. Can't stand any more of this. Let the stuff burn. What can we do?"

Steel-rigger Reader stepped over for the rifle, a grin on his face. "Did you suckers think I was going to risk my neck and yours over any deer? Get back on the wagon. I figured you'd weasel out. We're going into that fire and bring that engine out. You can run her better than I can, Norway. You'll get a reward maybe."

Reluctantly the men obeyed, realizing they had been tricked into one of Carlie Reader's daredevil games. The speeder wound slowly up the steeper grade into the choking pall of smoke, agony heightened by desperation. Only Carlie Reader felt free, his eyes and muscles alert with the excitement he smelled in the smoke.

Around a bend where the track leveled off before climbing the last grade into Camp 4, the men were suddenly aware of a lessening of the heat and thinning of the air. Ashes no longer blew down on them. Carlie Reader straightened and the speeder stopped.

"Wind's quit, or changed," he said, gun in hand. "Fire's still sizzling up there but if she was going like they said, she'd be all over here by now. Come on—let's get there."

Then the hot blast struck them full force as they switched back into the timber just below the camp. The cover here was scorching hot but still unburned, the course of the blaze being east along the ridge. Ahead of them, where the railroad track curved into the No. 4 clearing, all was a thick black smudge with stumps and trees glowing through it. From above, high up the mountainside, came the roaring hiss of the fire.

Dropping to the river bed out of the suffocating air, the four crawled up the wet rocks for a thousand feet and straight up the parched, desolated side of the ravine. At the top lay the ravished remains of the logging camp, great firs and cedars still burning like huge candles in the blackness. Low on the ground, visible only in the light from the flames, was a string of burning log cars, the Climax only a blacker shape.

"Yah, sure," one of the men said in scorn. "Save the lokey and get a reward. How was we such clobbering lunkheads to come up here with you, Carlie? Big shot—with a gun. You can't get a foot closer or the heat'll kill you."

Carlie Reader admitted it. Whatever plans he had were smothered in the heat and choking haze. He edged up, panting hard, and then fell back under the brow of the grade embankment.

"End of the trail, boys. But if I had some dynamite I'll bet I could stop that fire from going much farther. Maybe I could get around behind and up the mountain. Blow the top of that hill off into the face of the fire."

A familiar sound came up from below. The men scrambled down to the river again and followed it to where they had left the speeder. The sharp blasts of steam, the rattle and bang of steel on steel—no question about it now.

"It's the other Climax—and McGee! He never scuttled

out like he said. Look—he's got all of 'em—everybody!"

The locomotive chugged to a stop at the speeder and the loggers, laden with tools, were jumping down. Superintendent McGee hurried forward. He too had seen the wind had changed the course of the fire, that it was apparently stripping off the mountainside instead of racing downriver.

"Reader!" he shouted. "We've got a chance. We'll spread out straight up the hill here—cut a wide path—dig trenches."

The steel rigger threw his gun into the engine cab. "You got dynamite?"

"Sure. We'll blow out everything we can."

"Where is it?"

Carlie found the box, with fuses and caps. "Need another guy. Look, McGee—there's one chance. You'll never stop this fire with trenches and chopping out trees. See that big humpback hill up there? Blow that off and maybe the dirt will slide down over the fire and smother it. Just maybe. Anyway, nothing else to do. I'm going. Give me one man."

Logger McGee knew his man and did not try to hold him back. Three men came up, looking at the hill.

"Only one guy," Carlie Reader said. "And we got to hurry. All right, you—Frank Mussick. You're husky. Pack the box. I'll break trail. Let's go."

"Carlie," the superintendent called after him, "we'd have cleared out of the woods if you hadn't gone deer hunting. Make one big charge—and stay clear."

Carlie Reader may have heard him. He had already plunged like a hunted elk down the bank and up the river, big Frank Mussick with the dynamite stepping more carefully behind him. They had a sure destination—to circle the camp, get behind the fire, and ride the hump-back ridge above it.

That was their goal—and their grave. An hour later, with black sweat rolling off their faces as they swung axes and mattocks, the main body of fire fighters stiffened at the swelling "boom" somewhere above them. Rocks and debris came showering down.

"He rapped her all right," Homer McGee said quietly. "What a crazy daredevil. Wanted to get a deer and bring that Climax down. What a man."

The army of fighters kept slaving on in front of the flames. In the afternoon reinforcements came from the towns below the woods and the loggers slept exhaustedly on the banks of Hunting Creek. Whenever a man moved to drink water or cool his face, McGee thought it might be Carlie Reader or Frank Mussick returning. It was not. They never came back.

The fire raged for three more days and was then brought under control. Black as coal miners, dog-tired, the men straggled back to Camp 2—everyone except the two left somewhere up on Beard Mountain covered by a fall of dirt and all the glory Homer McGee could heap on them.

"That Carlie Reader," he always said. "He turned the tide that day. Folks want to give me credit for staying up there. Credit goes to that crazy steel rigger—the guy with the deer rifle and more courage than sense."

XVIII

Washington . . . 1915

SAMPSON OF THE TREETOPS

THE high climber worked a five-foot saw briskly through the cut. A few more minutes and the blade would reach the chopped area on the other side of the tree. The top would fall, the shank of the fir would sway, and he would come down, his job completed. That was what he was paid for. Danger? Thrills? The high climber shrugged. He got good money. How about letting it go at that?

A person on the ground looking up at this man taking the top off the towering fir, would not like to "let it go at that." The high climber was two hundred feet in the air, belted to the tree just under its bushy crown. He had reached this height on the tall, straight fir by hitching himself up by belt and climbing spurs to the first limb which he had then cut off. Another twenty feet up, he sawed away one or two more limbs. Twelve feet—more limbs. So, with the tree getting smaller and the workman cinching up his belt, he reached the dizzy extremity where he settled himself to cut off the top. If the high climber knew what he was doing it was a simple job. The daring lay in his doing it, the danger in that he might be careless or foolhardy.

The belt which held him to the tree was manila rope,

not wire rope as commonly used in high lead logging. The reason for using it was safety. Should the tree split when the top tumbled off, and spread, the rope binding the climber against the wood, a sharp blow of the ax would sever the fibers and release him. In this event only another heavy blow of the ax into the tree and a firm hold on the handle would prevent him from falling. And swinging even a three-pound ax fast enough to hold his weight was an acrobatic trick in itself.

Dangling at the high climber's waist as he climbed the tree was either the one-man saw or the ax, whichever he was not using at the moment. As he dug his spurs into the thick bark, first one foot and then the other, his body and tools swayed but were held securely by the rope belt. When he rose higher than the bight of the rope on the bark, he held his body close to the tree and skillfully flipped the rope eight or ten feet up, then climbed until it tightened again.

Reaching the point high on the trunk which the woods boss had indicated from below with a "Cut her about there," the high climber rested a moment or so, taking an eagle's-eye view of the great expanse of green forest carpet on the flanks of the mountain valley. He might grin down the skinned tree at visitors in camp or chatter back at a squirrel who had discovered his domain was being invaded. Then he would unhook the ax and go to work again, notching the small undercut and sawing in from the other side.

Above him like a canopy was the wide-spread, leafy crown of the fir, some thousand pounds of weight. As he sawed he kept the line well above the bottom of the under-cut so the falling top would not kick back and crush him.

He sawed easily but firmly, with workmanlike thrust and pull.

The top rustled and shuddered, then swayed quickly. As it fell the man loosened the belt and let it slip down as far as it would go, then in one flow of motion pushed his body away from the tree, jerked his spurs out of the bark, and dropped, the belt catching him and pulling him tight. Now the big green crown had snapped free and was hurtling earthward with a whistling *"whush."* The topped spar recoiled, whipping violently back and forth. Even before it stopped the high climber was on his way down, alternately flipping the belt and digging in his spurs. A dozen hitches and he was on the ground with a good appetite for supper. Another spar had been shaped up ready for rigging.

Philip Grabinski was a champion high climber of the northwest woods, in 1915 holding the exhibition record for scaling a spar tree 150 feet high in one minute and three seconds, lowering himself to the ground in eighteen seconds. An expert at topping fir trees, he was strong, daring, agile, and never in his logging life had a serious accident while "on top."

"I never figured my life was worth forty cents," Philip once told a foreman, "so I figured I might as well have some fun while I was at it." In point of fact his life was very valuable and he was careful with it. The bravado he showed was part of his gay, volatile nature. He knew there was less danger to high climbing than to setting chokers or tending hook on the ground. It was the spectacular show of it he liked—and the higher pay for less hours of work.

High climbing and high rigging became necessary after

the turn of the century when Western logging was moving into high production and the cry came down the line, "More logs! More logs!" To get more logs out of the woods and into the sawmills in less time, the logs had to be lifted off the ground. This was achieved through a succession of methods—from ground lead yarding by oxen, horses, and donkey engines to high lead or skyline systems.

These "highball" production methods involved the use of wire rope strung from spar tree to tail spar, sometimes a quarter of a mile apart, running through pulley-type blocks. Roller blocks or carriages moved along these cables, other wire lines hauling them from woods to logging engine and back to the woods again. Dangling from the moving blocks were the choker cables which carried the logs— several tons of them.

Spar trees were always fir, chosen for their tall, straight sturdiness. When they were topped and trimmed, resembling ships' masts with bark left on, guy lines were set to steady them under the great strain of the "flying" logs. Loading blocks were also rigged on the spar trees for piling the logs in cold decks or live storage piles or for hoisting them on railroad cars or gasoline trucks.

Philip Grabinski grew up in the Washington woods and all through his boyhood he had been fascinated by the feats of high climbers on the big trees and the steel riggers hanging lines and buckle guys after they had been topped. This was for him. He was inclined to "live dangerously" and in a day when there were no fast sport cars to race, no airplanes to fly, high climbing had just the right amount of spine-tingling risk he wanted. Chopping and sawing on the ground was for ordinary guys. High climbing was good circus stuff that made girls and greenhorns hold their breath and call him a hero.

But when he asked for a high climbing job, the woods boss sized him up quickly. He did not want a hero for a high climber. He wanted a good careful worker, a fellow who was looking for a good pay check, not glory. He grinned in a friendly fashion and told Phil to come back after he had some experience.

The eighteen-year-old boy got the experience by borrowing a set of climbing spurs and other gear from a friend of his father's who had fallen from a chickenhouse roof and sprained his leg. Phil practiced on short trees, climbed dead snags and then the tallest ones he could find. After three months he went back to the North Bend camp.

"You're the persistinest fella I seen lately," the woods boss told him, adding with a twinkle in his eye, "My regular climber disappeared. Heavy fog come in while he was up yonder and when it lifted, it must have took him along."

He started off into the woods, young Phil following at his heels. Pointing to a big fir, he said:

"There's your spar. Go to it. You're on the pay roll. Gimme a clean job and I'll keep you busy at this and hanging steel."

Young Grabinski saw the tree was about five feet in diameter, a hundred and eighty feet high. Now that he had a job, which was to climb this and cut the top off, the tree looked twice as big. He cinched up the rope belt, hooked ax and saw on it, passed over twenty feet of rope around the tree, and started up—"scared enough to be careful," he admitted later.

There were no limbs for sixty feet and he climbed at good speed, noting now the boss and several other loggers were standing near the yarding engine watching him. He lopped off the first branch and all the succeeding ones, which were smaller as he ascended. At the top he took a short rest, looking down on the great mass of timber and the antlike figures and jet of steam from the yarder. He felt a bit shaky. Seeing that he had plenty of rope and that the tree was less than two feet in diameter, he made himself feel easier by taking two loops around it.

When he started sawing and chopping he felt better and had the cut completed almost before he knew it. A few final saw thrusts and down came the top, jolting the tree only slightly, its sway short enough to be disappointing. He resisted an impulse to shout but did wave at the men below.

He felt like a veteran as he tackled his second tree the next day. It was a much larger and taller one—a longer and harder job. As he chopped at the wood his body kept swinging, spurs digging in deeper at each blow. The top cracked and snapped off but instead of pitching forward as it should, it struck another treetop and sprang backward over him.

Phil jerked desperately at the spikes but they held fast. He threw his arms around the tree and flattened his body against it. The falling weight cleared him but the spar leaped back, pulling his spurs free. The safety rope held him and after he dug the spurs in once more he could breathe easier. Coming down the tree this time, he knew his job was one to think about—not crow over.

As he grew proficient at his skill, Phil Grabinski learned

which type of rope was best—four strands of hemp over a soft wire core. This was strong enough to hold a man, yet if necessary it could be severed with one ax blow. He found that even well-placed ax slashes—parallel with the rope—sometimes got out of hand and one of the strands would be cut. This meant a pause for splicing. Sometimes while chopping, a spur would pull out and the ax cut the rope completely in two. He then had only his fingers of one hand to hold him while he drove in the ax for another hold and reset the rope.

The most danger occurred on windy days. He always worked with the wind at his back, the top falling with the wind, away from him. But it was in stormy weather that a tree was most likely to split. He might be chopping the undercut, the tree not yet sawed from the opposite side, and a sudden gust of wind would blow the top off, causing the tree to split.

This happened to high climber Grabinski at Camp 1 of St. Paul and Tacoma Lumber Company near Kapowsin, Washington. The top took a sudden dive with the wind, the trunk splitting evenly through the heart. When he saw the top falling, Phil loosened his rope and let it drop lower and scuttled squirrellike thirty feet down the tree. The split stopped just above his head.

High climbing and spar-tree topping proved unnecessary when the machine age took over the Northwest woods. Diesel skidders carried their own towers and diesel tractors instituted new methods—selective logging, the most efficient and least wasteful of all. So the exploits of high climbers became just another item to yarn about around the barrel stoves.

XIX

Washington . . . 1915

TRACKS TO THE CLOUDS

THE Western loggers were known for their courage and endurance under all kinds of working conditions. From the days of bull teams to the later ones of skylines and steel tower skidders, when logs were snatched from the woods and sent flying through the air to the landings, most of the loggers had backbone and sturdy hearts.

However this was not enough. Somewhere along the skid roads there had to be brains and inventive genius. Half the timber in the West would still be standing if ways and means had not been devised to get it out. Thousands upon thousands of acres of Douglas fir, Western red cedar, spruce, and hemlock were too high in the mountains, too low in the swamps, too far across the gullies.

To bring in such inaccessible stuff some of the loggers had to design water flumes, high railroad trestles, and wire rope systems, and build them quickly enough and cheaply enough to make the job profitable. None of the engineering feats were more spectacular than the incline railroads where tracks went "straight up the mountainside."

"Hugh," the general manager of the Clear Lake Lumber Company said one day in 1915, "I want you to build us an incline. We've got a lot of timber on the west side

of the lower Haystack but the lay is too steep to switchback a railroad or even bring the logs down by slack line.
How is that incline working—the one you built for Ebey
at Arlington?"

"Right well, chief," replied Hugh Sessons, who had
been building railroads in the Washington woods for a
number of years. "The one at Hamilton too—Dempsey's.
He's using that new block car I figured out."

"Well, you're the man I want. We'll take a run up to
Camp 4 with the boys in the morning and look the situation over. Trip leaves at six-thirty. You'll be here?"

Sessons nodded, the geared wheels in his head already
beginning to turn. He knew the country along the Skagit
River very well. He had fished the creeks that fed it clear
up to the snow line and had climbed Haystack Mountain,
a rocky cliff standing four thousand feet above sea level.
He knew the timber area the superintendent had referred
to. No question about it—the grade was heavy.

He was back at the Clear Lake sawmill in the foggy,
predawn darkness. The Shay locomotive was panting at
the head of ten empty log cars and the "crummy," the
work car in which the logging crew rode to work. He
climbed in and joined the men crowding the slab-burner
fashioned from a four-hundred-pound grease drum.

"It's Hugh Sessons," a voice said and a lanky figure in a
dirty canvas cap and jacket waved a hand. "Mr. Sessons,
you ought to be on the head end where good engine men
ride." The logger tucked a finger of "snoose," dipped from
a small round box, under his lower lip.

"Rather be here with the elite folks, Hobie. Besides, the
Old Man is in on this. New steel."

"Incline?"

"Maybe. We'll take a look first."

The car was filled with over fifty men when the super-intendent arrived. The trip pulled out with the brakeman swinging his lantern and riding the open steps until the Shay had cleared the drying yard. The main line ran up Day Creek through rock cuts and over bridges, climbing steadily. As the grade grew heavier, the crummy rolled and rattled, the squeal of wheels on the curves muffled by the thickened fog. Seven miles later the sky began to gray and Day Creek was a thin silver ribbon a thousand feet down in the gorge.

When the train stopped, Camp 4 opened up as a clut-tered clearing in a light cover of timber, the air cleaned of mist by the rising sun. To the south lay nothing but stumps and slash where a strip had been logged. The men streamed off the car and headed for the donkey engine, log landing, and shops. As Hugh Sessons followed the Old Man around a sixty-foot cold deck of logs into the virgin timber east of the camp, the Shay was switching cars in a fury of steam.

The railroad builder had brought no instruments and he needed none. Their use would come on the next trip— to survey and lay grade on blueprints. It was enough now that he get a general view of the terrain.

The two men skirted the flat timber area and mounted the slopes until they reached a saddle. Beyond this the flanks of the mountain presented an almost perpendicular barrier. The big trees grew straight up but seemed to cling precariously by exposed roots. In Hugh Sesson's eye the main line track was already laid in a series of switch-

backs to the foot of another rise which the superintendent
pointed out as the section he wanted to tap first. His head
was tipped far back as he gazed upward.

"She's wicked. About fifty per cent, I'd say, right here."

"Close to it," Sessions agreed. "But grade don't matter
if other conditions are right and the snubber is powered
heavy enough, and the block car built right. I've got ideas
to improve the last one I built. Let's go up."

By midafternoon he had made his preliminary survey.
The slope was too long for one unbroken stretch of track.
So he would set the incline on two pitches and farther
north. That would ease the strain on cables and drums.
The first pitch would have to run under a main line
trestle on the switchback unless . . . The problem remained unanswered. The solution depended on other factors. But the answers were there somewhere.

Within ten days a grade camp was established and work
began. Main line track was laid by switchbacks to the foot
of the incline grade. The hill was logged and brushed out.
An area at the top of it was cleared for the site of the new
Camp 4, the old one to be abandoned when the incline
went into operation.

And ninety days later it did. The test trip hauled up
two empty cars and lowered one hand-loaded with track-
laying equipment. The next took up part of the camp
buildings. After that a Shay lokey was hauled up and two
full cars of logs were lowered. The Clear Lake officials con-
gratulated Hugh Sessions for adding another successful
incline to his list of accomplishments.

"You wait now," the builder cautioned them. "There's
still some kinks to shake out. Tomorrow we'll move all

the rest of the camp to the top—with all the men. I'll tell
you then if she's right."

Up the incline the next morning went thirteen cars
with all the equipment and workers of Camp 4. On the
block car at the head of the string rode Hugh Sessons. This
car was the key to the operation—his own invention on
which he was continually improving.

When the trip was ready to start, he threw a lever on
the side of the block car to signal the operator of the snubbing machine—a big donkey engine out of sight at the
top of the grade, almost half a mile up the mountain. The
heavy cable, running down from the snubber at the left
of the track, tightened against its idler blocks, and as it
passed through a giant sheave mounted on the block car
and out to the right, running up the grade to the engine
drums, the block car and the thirteen others behind it
moved slowly up the incline. As the cable wound around
the drums, the indirect pull on the big block drew the
load up.

The cars were rising slowly and steadily, blocks and
pulleys keeping tension on the wire ropes. Hugh Sessons
watched every movement and listened to every sound.
When the train had surmounted the first pitch of 42 per
cent, it leveled off to some extent, then began the larger
and steeper climb of 48 per cent. Twenty-four hundred
feet up the snubbing engine, operating like a mine hoist,
came into view, her stack belching wood smoke, a stream
of water playing on the brake bands.

When the train flattened out on the level ground of
new Camp 4, the railroad builder nodded to the foreman.
"She'll do. Only one thing, Pete. Don't ever lower more

than two loaded cars at a time. Got a bucket of coffee in the shack?"

Two cars of logs, then, was the lowering limit. Twenty tons of timber. The snubbing machine had almost unlimited power but Hugh Sessions said two cars was the safe limit. Cables could break. The big block traveling on the first car could get off balance and foul up the lines. Steel rails could spring apart. All these were things that could happen, but the Camp 4 incline looked good.

Within three weeks production was heading into full capacity. Hugh Sessions had gone home well satisfied with his work and the sawmill began calling for more logs. Clear Lake was Washington's largest inland mill, cutting a million feet a day. Demand for lumber was unceasing.

The Camp 4 foreman was under pressure and only human. Lowering two cars at a time was all right but putting on three would speed things up 50 per cent. The cold and hot decks of logs were growing faster than the incline could take them away. "Run three cars in there after this," he ordered the locomotive engineer.

The operator at the snubber controls knew where his orders came from. When three cars of logs were coupled to the block car, he shot steam into the pistons and the drums unwound foot upon foot of two-inch steel rope. Thirty tons of fir logs settled themselves to a half-mile descent to the track switch at the bottom of the incline. One man rode the lower car to signal back any trouble.

There were four logs on this car, the bottom two snug against the side bunks, the top two holding them down. The loading theory was that if a log rolled off it would drop harmlessly in the brush alongside the track and the

lowering would not be halted. And with the wheels rolling smoothly, steel on steel, the speed not five miles an
hour, how could a log roll off? One never had.

But this time one did—one of the top logs on the lower
car. Off balance when the trip started, one end swung out
slowly on the first pitch and the entire log rolled off. The
logger standing on the front of the car let it pass over
him and watched it roll.

Then the trouble started. When the log hit the ground
it bounded back from a stump, one end pivoting in front
of the car wheels. The descending car pushed the log down
the track for a few feet and then bucked up over it, hurling the load man to one side and spilling the other three
logs to the opposite side, the now empty car slewing sideways and jamming into the roadbed.

The weight of the next two cars came crashing down
on top of it and the seven logs they carried went sprawling
in all directions, sliding and tumbling down the track
in an avalanche of dirt and rocks. By a miracle it all passed
over the body of the logger lying low in the brush. He
jumped up and grabbed the signal lever on the block car.
When the cables stopped, all four cars were piled on sides
and ends over the twisted rails.

It was a minor accident and the only one that occurred
on the Camp 4 incline. On several others, cables slipped
and broke, killing men and ruining equipment. In another case, a donkey engine was being raised up the incline and got away from its handlers, plunging down the
slope to smash itself into a mass of useless steel.

But on this Clear Lake incline no lives were lost, no
equipment seriously damaged. In a week logs were being

lowered again and the experience was charged to too much speed in an effort to feed the hungry hoppers of the sawmill. And in no way was the accident a reflection on the ingenuity of Hugh Sessons. His "tracks to the clouds" were a highly successful aid to logging in Washington's high country, a fine tribute to his engineering skill.

BOOKS FOR FURTHER READING

Ralph W. Andrews. *Glory Days of Logging*. Seattle: Superior Publishing Co., 1956.

——. *This Was Logging*. Seattle: Superior Publishing Co., 1954.

——. *This was Sawmilling*. Seattle: Superior Publishing Co., 1957.

Archie Binns. *The Timber Beast*. New York: Charles Scribner's Sons, 1944.

Donald H. Clark. *18 Men and a Horse*. Seattle: Metropolitan Press, 1949.

Edwin T. Coman, Jr., and Helen M. Gibbs. *Time, Tide, and Timber*. Stanford: Stanford University Press, 1949.

H. J. Cox. *Random Lengths*. Eugene, Ore.: 1949.

Stewart Holbrook. *Green Commonwealth*. Seattle: Dogwood Press, 1945.

——. *Half Century in the Timber*. Seattle: Dogwood Press, 1945.

——. *Holy Old Mackinaw*. New York: The Macmillan Company, 1938.

Paul Hosmer. *Now We're Loggin'*. Portland, Ore.: Metropolitan Press, 1930.

Jack McNairn and Jerry MacMullen. *Ships of the Redwood Coast*. Stanford: Stanford University Press, 1945.

Murray C. Morgan. *The Last Wilderness*. New York: The Viking Press, Inc., 1955.

James Stevens. *Paul Bunyan*. New York: Alfred A. Knopf, Inc., 1925.

INDEX

Acme (schooner), 51-55
Alaska, discovery of gold, 106
Anderson, A. H., 106-107
Astor, John Jacob, 34
Astoria, Oregon, 34, 133, 135-136
Australia, lumber sent to, 44, 46

Bark-peeling, 78-79
Beard Mountain, 152
Beasley, Tod, 32
Beavis, John, 134
Benson, Simon, 134-140
Benson Timber Company, 134, 140
"Big Four, The," 20-29
Birmingham (bark), 30-31, 33
Black Mountain, Oregon, 115
Blackwell, C. W. ("Cy"), 109-113
Blakely railroad, 102-107
Bodega Bay, 21-23, 26
Brand on logs, 157-158
Breen, Ed, 124
Brown, E. S., 43, 45
Bull teams, 26, 29, 79-80, 108-111, 154
  drivers or "skinners," 108-113
  replaced by donkey engines, 156-157

Camps, logging, 118, 145-147, 150
Cape Flattery, 46, 152
Carney, "Whitewater" Jim, 141-151
Cascade Mountains, 152
Cathlamet, Oregon, 134

Cedar Lake, Wash., 180-186
Cedar logs, 43, 108, 152, 180
Chehalis Boom, 153, 158, 160
Chutes for logs, 114-122
  loading ships by, 76
  Sugar Pines, 114, 119-122
Clear Lake Lumber Company, 180
Columbia (passenger steamer), 55-56
Columbia River, 34, 133, 136, 139, 152
Converse Basin, 93-101
Cook, John, 114-122
Cook and Company, 120-122
Coos Bay, 35, 37-39, 109
Cornwall, Neil, 129-132
Crockett, Calif., 74

Dams, splash, 110
Derricks, floating, 136-137
Diesel skidders, 179
"Dog holes" of California, 23, 50
Dolbeer, John, 81, 106, 155-157
Donkey engines, 81-82, 106, 156-157
Douglas fir, 34, 40, 140, 152, 180
Drives, *see* Log drives
Duff, Wiley, 14-15, 18

Ellsworth, Clem F., 63-72, 97
"Ellsworth's Folly," 65-72
Emerson, George H., 40
Empire City, Oregon, 36-39
Engines, donkey, 81-82, 106, 155-157

Eureka, Calif., 51
Eva (riverboat), 123-132
Evenson, Ole J., 134-140

Fastabend, John A., 135-136, 138
Felling trees, 77-78
Fir trees, 34, 40, 108, 140, 152, 180
Floods, 153, 158
Flumes, lumber, 64-72, 97-101
  boats, 68-72, 97-101
Forbes, Billy, 104
Ford, Jerome, 21, 23-24, 26-28
Forest fires, 91-92, 122, 162-172
  dynamiting hillside, 167-169
Forests, 33, 42, 152
Fort Bragg, Calif., 75, 81-82
Fort Ross, 17, 74-75
Foster, Charles, 44

Gardiner, Oregon, 40, 123-132
Gardiner Lumber Company, 124
Gin Pole John, 143-144, 147, 150
Gold Rush, 20-29, 30-32, 63, 106
Grabinski, Philip, 175-176
Grays Harbor, Wash., 40, 44, 109,
  110, 152, 158-160

Harlan, Jacob, 14-18
Harris, Captain William H., 36
Hawaii, lumber sent to, 44
Hemlock, 152, 180
High climbers, 173-179
"Highball" operations, 162, 176
Hinsdale, George, 124-125
Holbrook, Stewart, 10
Hong Kong, lumber sent to, 47
Hood Canal, 43, 107
Hook tender, 112
Horse teams, 105-106, 108, 116-118
Humboldt Bay, 51-52, 56

Hume, George, 101
Hunter, James, 76, 81
Hunting Creek, 162-172
Huntley, Orman, 104

Indians, 35, 45, 47-49, 154
  raids, 47-49

Jackscrews, 79, 80
James, log, 121-122, 142, 149
Jewett, W. F., 123-132
Johnson, C. Russel, 73-82
Julius Pringle (brig), 43-46

Kasten, William, 23
Keller, Captain J. P., 44-49
Kesterson, Ben, 153-154
Kesterson, Ed, 154-155, 158
Kings River, Calif., 93-101
Klamathon, Oregon, 114-122

Lane, C. D., 107
Lansing, David, 21, 23-27
Leeds, J. B., 124
Lindquist, Sven, 127-132
Log drives, 147-151, 155
  bateaux for, 147, 149-150
  clothes for, 145
  start of, 148
Log jams, 121-122, 142, 149
Luse, Harry, 36-39

McGee, Homer, 162-172
McSherry, Charlie, 142-144
Mahoney, Dapper Dan, 142-146,
  151
Maine expeditions, 30, 42, 44, 49,
  63, 124-125

Mason Country Central railroad, 105
Mayfair (schooner), 57-62
Meiggs, Harry, 21-24, 28
Mendocino area, 23-29
"dog holes," 50-62
Mendocino Saw Mills, 29
Millwood, Calif., 96-97
Mining ventures, 63, 120-121
Moore, A. D., 93-101
Moran, Captain Peter, 55-56
Mount Shasta country, 63
Mussick, Frank, 171-172

National Steamship Company, 82
Navarro River, 75
New Kamilche, Wash., 103-104
North Bend, Oregon, 41

Olsen, Charles Oluf, 5-6, 10
Olsen, Captain "Midnight," 50-62
Olympia Peninsula, Wash., 42
Ontario (brig), 25-27
Oxen, 111, *see also* Bull teams

Pettigrew, Archie, 89-91
Pirating of logs, 157-158
Pit River, Calif., 141-151
Ponderosa pine, 97
Peninsular Railroad, 106
Phoenix Logging Company, 107
Pope, Andrew, 44, 46
Pope and Talbot enterprises, 43-49, 83, 92, 103
Port Blakely, 102-107
Port Gamble, Wash., 46-49, 84, 103
Port Ludlow, Wash., 83-85, 89, 103
Port Orford cedar, 39
Portland, Oregon, 34, 134
Puget Mill Company, 44-49

Puget Sound, 43-49, 83, 102-107
logging railroad, 103-107

Rafts, log, 121-122, 133-140
Benson, 134
Railroads, logging, 95-96, 103-107, 134, 136, 166
block cars, 181, 183-185
engines, 105, 107, 184
inclined, 180-186
narrow gauge, 117-118
right-of-way, 103
Reader, Charlie, 167-169
Reagan, Tam, 89-91
Redding and Big Bend Lumber Co., 143
Redwood Manufacturing Co., 29
Redwoods, 13-19
age of, 21-22
felling, 77-78
first cuttings, 13-19
loading cargoes of, 50-62
logging, 28, 77-82
Mendocino area, 23-29
peeling the bark, 78-79
qualities of, 16
Sierra Nevada, 93-101
size of, 16, 22, 74-75
stands of, 75
Reed, Mark, 107
Renton, Captain William, 44, 102-107
River men, 141-151
Robertson, Captain Hugh, 134-135
Rope belt, 174, 177, 179
Russian colonies, 17, 74

Sacramento River, 141
St. Paul and Tacoma Lumber Co., 179

San Francisco, 16-17, 20, 29, 73-74
  Gold Rush, 20, 22, 30-32, 52
Sanger, Calif., 99-100
Satsop Railroad, 103, 105-106
Satsop River, 153, 157
Saw mills, 28-29, 39
  machinery, 23, 25, 36, 37, 46
  Puget Sound, 43-44
  steam, 37-38
Schafer Brothers, 153-161
Schutt, Harold, 10
Seattle, Wash., 156
Selective logging, 179
Sequoia Lake dam, 98
Sesma, Calif., 65-67, 71, 72
Sessons, Hugh, 181-186
Seymour, Louis, 10, 126
Shasta Country, 64
Shingles, 17-19, 75
Ships for transporting lumber, 25,
  39, 44, 46, 49, 55-62
Shipyards, 32, 39, 83
Sierra Nevada Mountains, 93
Simpson, Asa, 30-41
Simpson, George, 104
Simpson, Joseph, 104
Simpson, Louis, 36-37
Simpson, Captain Robert W., 36,
  39
Simpson, Sol G., 102-107
Simpson Logging Company, 106-
  107
Sitka spruce, 34
Skid greaser, 109, 154
Skid roads, 104-105, 108-110, 112,
  154
Smith, Hiram C., 93-101
Smith, Captain Stephen, 21-22, 26
Soule, Captain Tom, 158-161
Spar trees, 175-176, 179

Spruce logs, 34, 108, 180
Starr, A. D., 74-76
Steel tower skidders, 180
Stewart, Calvin, 76, 81
Stewart, E. J., 10
Strait of Juan de Fuca, 42, 152
Sugar pines, 97, 114-122
Sutcliff, George, 129-130
Swamper, 79, 110
Swift, Richard, 13, 15, 17
Sutter's mills, 31, 36

Talbot, Captain William C., 42-49
Topping fir trees, 173-175
Tug boats, 83-89, 158-159
  hijacking of, 83-89
  towing rafts, 139
Tyee (tug), 83-89

Umpqua River, 35-36, 40, 123, 125
Union Lumber Company, 73, 82

Wagon trains, 97
Walker, Cyrus, 43, 45, 47, 49, 83-92
Waste of trees, 95
Water conduit for lumber, 65-66
Weather, 152-153, 162
Western red cedar, 34, 152, 180
Wheels for logging, 117-118
White City by-the-Sea, 123-132
Williams, Edward C., 20-24, 28-29
Wilson, Buck, 166
Wilson, Sam, 127-128
Winchester Bay, Oregon, 123, 125

Yakima (tug), 87-88